M000019192

TEACHER'S PET PUBLICATIONS

PUZZLE PACK
for
The Joy Luck Club

based on the book by
Amy Tan

Written by
William T. Collins

© 2005 Teacher's Pet Publications
All Rights Reserved

Copyrighted

The materials in this packet are copyrighted
by Teacher's Pet Publications, Inc.

These pages may be duplicated by the purchaser
for use in the purchaser's own classroom.

Copying any of these materials and distributing them
for any other purpose is a violation of the copyright laws.

© 2005 Teacher's Pet Publications, Inc.
www.tpet.com

INTRODUCTION

If you already own the LitPlan for this title, this Puzzle Pack will refresh your Unit Resource Materials and Vocabulary Resource Materials sections plus give you additional materials you can substitute into the tests.If you do not already have a complete LitPlan, these pages will give you some supplemental materials to use with your own plan. There are two main groups of materials: one set for unit words (such as characters' names, symbols, places, etc.) and one set for vocabulary words associated with the book.

WORD LIST

There is a word list for both the unit words and the vocabulary words. These lists show you which words are being used in the materials and the clues or definitions being used for those words. You may want to give students a word list with clues/definitions to help them, or you may want students to only have a word list (without clues/definitions) if you want them to work a little harder. Both are available for duplication. The word lists can also be your "calling key" for the bingo games.

FILL IN THE BLANK AND MATCHING

There are 4 each of the fill in the blank and matching worksheets for both the unit and vocabulary words. These pages can be used either as extra worksheets for students or as objective parts of a unit test. They can be done individually if students need extra help or as a whole class activity to review the material covered.

MAGIC SQUARES

The magic squares not only reinforce the material covered but also work on reasoning and math skills. Many teachers have told us that their students really enjoy doing these!

WORD SEARCH PUZZLES

The word search words go in all directions, as indicated on your answer keys. Two of the word search puzzles have the clues listed rather than the words. This makes the puzzle a little more difficult, but it reinforces the material better. Two word search puzzles have words only for students who find the clue puzzles too difficult.

CROSSWORD PUZZLES

Both unit and vocabulary word sections have 4 crossword puzzles.

BINGO CARDS

There are 32 individual bingo cards for the unit words and 32 individual bingo cards for the vocabulary words. You can use your word list as a "call list," calling the words at random and marking them off of your list as you go, or you could use the flash cards by cutting them apart and drawing the words at random from a hat (or box or whatever). To make a better review, you might ask for the definition and spelling of each word as you call it out–or you could call out the definitions and have students tell you the words they need to look for on the puzzle.

JUGGLE LETTERS

The vocabulary juggle letter game is intended to help students learn the spellings of the words. One sheet has the definitions listed on it as an extra help for students who need it or to reinforce the definitions if you choose to do so.

FLASH CARDS

We've included a set of vocabulary flash cards you can duplicate, cut, and fold for your students. Some teachers make a few sets for general use by the class; others make a set for each student. Some teachers duplicate them for each student and have the students cut & fold their own. You can cut out just the words and put them in a hat, have each student pick out one word and write the definition and a sentence for that word. Students then swap words and papers, with the next student adding a sentence of his own under the last one. You can have students swap as many times as you like. Each time the student will read the sentences written prior to his own and then add a sentence. You can cut out the words and definitions separately and play "I Have; Who Has?" Each student in the room draws a word and definition. The first student says, "I have (the name of the word). Who has the definition?" The student with the definition reads it then says, "I have (the name of the vocabulary word she has). Who has the definition?" The round continues until all words and definitions have been given.

Copyrighted

Joy Luck Club Word List

No.	Word	Clue/Definition
1.	ARCHITECT	Lena's profession
2.	ARNOLD	He tormented Lena.
3.	ART	Lindo taught Waverly the ___ of invisible strength.
4.	BIBLE	It is under the table leg in the kitchen.
5.	BING	He drowned.
6.	BLOOD	Ying-ying got it on her clothes.
7.	BOAT	Ying-ying fell off the ___ and got separated from her family.
8.	BRIGHTNESS	Festival of Pure ___
9.	CANDLE	It was supposed to be lit at both ends and kept burning all night.
10.	CHANG	Necklace made of red jade
11.	CHESS	Waverly's game
12.	CHILD	'Pleading ___'; Jing-mei's piano piece
13.	CHINA	Waverly wants to go there for her second honeymoon.
14.	CHOU	Sleep; visit Mr. ___
15.	CHUNG	Piano teacher
16.	CLAIR	Ying-ying St. ___: Lena's mother
17.	COLD	If the lips are gone, the teeth will be ___.
18.	COOKIE	An-mei and Lindo met at the ___ factory.
19.	CRAB	One with a lost leg on Chinese New Year is a bad sign.
20.	DOUBLE	___ Face
21.	FAITH	Rose defines it as an illusion that one is somehow in control.
22.	FOUND	Ying-ying's wish was to be ___.
23.	FOUR	___ Directions
24.	FRANCISCO	Jong family lived there: San ___
25.	GATES	The Twenty-six Malignant ___
26.	GLASS	The beads of An-mei's necklace from Second Wife were made of this.
27.	GRAVE	For An-mei to say her mother's name was to spit on her father's ___.
28.	HAROLD	Lena's husband
29.	HEAVEN	Jong family hill: Three Steps to ___
30.	HSU	An-mei ___; Rose ___ Jordan
31.	JANICE	Rose's sister
32.	JEWELRY	Matchmaker suggested Lindo take off all her ___ to be better balanced.
33.	JOY	___ Luck Club
34.	JUNE	Jing-mei's American name
35.	KINDS	Two ___
36.	KWEILIN	Original setting for JLC meetings
37.	LAUPO	Waverly's neighbor who played chess with her
38.	LEFTOVERS	Meaning of 'yu' in Tyan-yu's name
39.	LENA	Ying-ying's daughter
40.	LIFESAVERS	They took the place of the white knight and black pawn.
41.	LINDO	Waverly's mother
42.	LUCKY	The women hoped to be ___ and that was their only joy.
43.	MAGAZINES	Jing-mei's mother looked at these for stories about exceptional children.
44.	MAGPIES	The eggs from the turtle's beak produced 7 of these.
45.	MAN	Moon Lady became one.
46.	MEIMEI	Waverly's family called her this.
47.	MOLE	Proof of the rotting marriage
48.	MOON	___ Lady
49.	NINGPO	Where An-mei's family lived in China
50.	OPIUM	Substance First Wife used
51.	PIANO	Instrument Jing-mei played

Copyrighted

No.	Word	Clue/Definition
52.	POPO	An-mei's name for her grandmother.
53.	QUALITY	Best ___
54.	RED	Color of the candle
55.	RICE	___ Husband
56.	RICH	Mr. Shields
57.	RING	Rose's mother threw her blue sapphire one into the water.
58.	RULES	___ of the Game
59.	SHANGHAI	Jing-mei goes there to find her sisters.
60.	SHOSHANA	Waverly's daughter
61.	SHOU	Having no respect for ancestors or family
62.	SHOUT	On the third day after her mother died, An-mei learned to do this.
63.	SOUP	It burned An-mei the night her mother returned.
64.	SUN	Moon Lady's husband lives there.
65.	SUYUAN	Jing-mei's mother: ___ Woo
66.	TAITAI	Huang ___; Tyan-yu's mother
67.	TAIYUAN	Lindo's village
68.	TAN	Author Amy
69.	TAO	This society gave Waverly her second chess set.
70.	TED	Rose's husband
71.	TICKETS	A Pair Of ___
72.	TREES	Waiting Between The ___
73.	TURTLE	It ate the tears.
74.	TYANYU	Lindo's husband via the matchmaker
75.	VINCENT	He actually got the chess set for Christmas.
76.	VOICE	___ From the Wall
77.	WAVERLY	Lindo Jong's daughter
78.	WOOD	Without ___
79.	WUSHI	Where Ying-ying grew up
80.	WUTSING	He owned house where An-mei and her mother lived.
81.	YAN	An-mei's personal maid: ___ Chung

Copyrighted

Joy Luck Club Fill In The Blanks 1

_____   1. Proof of the rotting marriage

_____   2. This society gave Waverly her second chess set.

_____   3. Substance First Wife used

_____   4. Meaning of 'yu' in Tyan-yu's name

_____   5. Best ___

_____   6. Waverly's daughter

_____   7. Rose's sister

_____   8. Two ___

_____   9. Necklace made of red jade

_____   10. Where Ying-ying grew up

_____   11. Jing-mei's mother: ___ Woo

_____   12. Ying-ying got it on her clothes.

_____   13. Lindo's village

_____   14. The beads of An-mei's necklace from Second Wife were
                               made of this.

                           15. The women hoped to be ___ and that was their only joy.

_____   16. The Twenty-six Malignant ___

_____   17. Ying-ying fell off the ___ and got separated from her family.

_____   18. An-mei and Lindo met at the ___ factory.

_____   19. Jong family hill: Three Steps to ___

_____   20. An-mei's name for her grandmother.

Copyrighted

MOLE	1. Proof of the rotting marriage
TAO	2. This society gave Waverly her second chess set.
OPIUM	3. Substance First Wife used
LEFTOVERS	4. Meaning of 'yu' in Tyan-yu's name
QUALITY	5. Best ___
SHOSHANA	6. Waverly's daughter
JANICE	7. Rose's sister
KINDS	8. Two ___
CHANG	9. Necklace made of red jade
WUSHI	10. Where Ying-ying grew up
SUYUAN	11. Jing-mei's mother: ___ Woo
BLOOD	12. Ying-ying got it on her clothes.
TAIYUAN	13. Lindo's village
GLASS	14. The beads of An-mei's necklace from Second Wife were made of this.
LUCKY	15. The women hoped to be ___ and that was their only joy.
GATES	16. The Twenty-six Malignant ___
BOAT	17. Ying-ying fell off the ___ and got separated from her family.
COOKIE	18. An-mei and Lindo met at the ___ factory.
HEAVEN	19. Jong family hill: Three Steps to ___
POPO	20. An-mei's name for her grandmother.

Copyrighted

_____

_____

_____

_____

_____

_____

_____

_____

_____

_____

_____

_____

_____

_____

_____

_____

_____

_____

1. It burned An-mei the night her mother returned.

2. It was supposed to be lit at both ends and kept burning all night.

3. Rose defines it as an illusion that one is somehow in control.

4. Rose's husband

5. Waverly's daughter

6. Lindo's husband via the matchmaker

7. Author Amy

8. Best ___

9. Mr. Shields

10. Substance First Wife used

11. Waverly wants to go there for her second honeymoon.

12. Lena's husband

13. Ying-ying St. ___: Lena's mother

14. Rose's sister

15. Jing-mei's American name

16. An-mei ___; Rose ___ Jordan

17. Waverly's game

18. 'Pleading ___'; Jing-mei's piano piece

19. Ying-ying fell off the ___ and got separated from her family.

20. ___ Directions

Copyrighted

Joy Luck Club Fill In The Blanks 2 Answer Key

SOUP

CANDLE

FAITH

TED

SHOSHANA

TYANYU

TAN

QUALITY

RICH

OPIUM

CHINA

HAROLD

CLAIR

JANICE

JUNE

HSU

CHESS

CHILD

BOAT

FOUR

1. It burned An-mei the night her mother returned.

2. It was supposed to be lit at both ends and kept burning all night.

3. Rose defines it as an illusion that one is somehow in control.

4. Rose's husband

5. Waverly's daughter

6. Lindo's husband via the matchmaker

7. Author Amy

8. Best ___

9. Mr. Shields

10. Substance First Wife used

11. Waverly wants to go there for her second honeymoon.

12. Lena's husband

13. Ying-ying St. ___: Lena's mother

14. Rose's sister

15. Jing-mei's American name

16. An-mei ___; Rose ___ Jordan

17. Waverly's game

18. 'Pleading ___'; Jing-mei's piano piece

19. Ying-ying fell off the ___ and got separated from her family.

20. ___ Directions

Copyrighted

_____   1. ___ of the Game

_____   2. An-mei and Lindo met at the ___ factory.

_____   3. Best ___

_____   4. Huang ___; Tyan-yu's mother

_____   5. Sleep; visit Mr. ___

_____   6. It is under the table leg in the kitchen.

_____   7. He tormented Lena.

_____   8. If the lips are gone, the teeth will be ___.

_____   9. Rose's husband

_____   10. The Twenty-six Malignant ___

_____   11. Mr. Shields

_____   12. Without ___

_____   13. Festival of Pure ___

_____   14. The eggs from the turtle's beak produced 7 of these.

_____   15. Proof of the rotting marriage

_____   16. Rose defines it as an illusion that one is somehow in control.

_____   17. Substance First Wife used

_____   18. Waiting Between The ___

_____   19. An-mei's name for her grandmother.

_____   20. He owned house where An-mei and her mother lived.

Copyrighted

Joy Luck Club Fill In The Blanks 3 Answer Key

RULES   1. ___ of the Game

COOKIE   2. An-mei and Lindo met at the ___ factory.

QUALITY   3. Best ___

TAITAI   4. Huang ___; Tyan-yu's mother

CHOU   5. Sleep; visit Mr. ___

BIBLE   6. It is under the table leg in the kitchen.

ARNOLD   7. He tormented Lena.

COLD   8. If the lips are gone, the teeth will be ___.

TED   9. Rose's husband

GATES   10. The Twenty-six Malignant ___

RICH   11. Mr. Shields

WOOD   12. Without ___

BRIGHTNESS   13. Festival of Pure ___

MAGPIES   14. The eggs from the turtle's beak produced 7 of these.

MOLE   15. Proof of the rotting marriage

FAITH   16. Rose defines it as an illusion that one is somehow in control.

OPIUM   17. Substance First Wife used

TREES   18. Waiting Between The ___

POPO   19. An-mei's name for her grandmother.

WUTSING   20. He owned house where An-mei and her mother lived.

Copyrighted

_____   1. Original setting for JLC meetings

_____   2. An-mei's personal maid: ___ Chung

_____   3. Lindo Jong's daughter

_____   4. Where Ying-ying grew up

_____   5. Substance First Wife used

_____   6. Waverly's neighbor who played chess with her

_____   7. Where An-mei's family lived in China

_____   8. It burned An-mei the night her mother returned.

_____   9. ___ Lady

_____   10. He drowned.

_____   11. ___ Directions

_____   12. ___ Luck Club

_____   13. Lena's husband

_____   14. Waverly's family called her this.

_____   15. 'Pleading ___'; Jing-mei's piano piece

_____   16. ___ Face

_____   17. Author Amy

_____   18. It ate the tears.

_____   19. Ying-ying fell off the ___ and got separated from her family.

_____   20. ___ of the Game

Copyrighted

Joy Luck Club Fill In The Blanks 4 Answer Key

KWEILIN   1. Original setting for JLC meetings

YAN   2. An-mei's personal maid: ___ Chung

WAVERLY   3. Lindo Jong's daughter

WUSHI   4. Where Ying-ying grew up

OPIUM   5. Substance First Wife used

LAUPO   6. Waverly's neighbor who played chess with her

NINGPO   7. Where An-mei's family lived in China

SOUP   8. It burned An-mei the night her mother returned.

MOON   9. ___ Lady

BING   10. He drowned.

FOUR   11. ___ Directions

JOY   12. ___ Luck Club

HAROLD   13. Lena's husband

MEIMEI   14. Waverly's family called her this.

CHILD   15. 'Pleading ___'; Jing-mei's piano piece

DOUBLE   16. ___ Face

TAN   17. Author Amy

TURTLE   18. It ate the tears.

BOAT   19. Ying-ying fell off the ___ and got separated from her family.

RULES   20. ___ of the Game

Copyrighted

Joy Luck Club Matching 1

___ 1. BLOOD   A. It is under the table leg in the kitchen.

___ 2. LINDO   B. It burned An-mei the night her mother returned.

___ 3. TAN   C. Rose's sister

___ 4. HSU   D. Ying-ying's daughter

___ 5. LEFTOVERS   E. An-mei ___; Rose ___ Jordan

___ 6. SHOU   F. This society gave Waverly her second chess set.

___ 7. TURTLE   G. ___ Lady

___ 8. CHINA   H. Mr. Shields

___ 9. PIANO   I. Ying-ying got it on her clothes.

___10. SHANGHAI   J. Original setting for JLC meetings

___11. FOUR   K. Meaning of 'yu' in Tyan-yu's name

___12. TAO   L. Lena's profession

___13. MOON   M. Waverly wants to go there for her second honeymoon.

___14. KWEILIN   N. It ate the tears.

___15. TAIYUAN   O. Instrument Jing-mei played

___16. LENA   P. Jing-mei goes there to find her sisters.

___17. SOUP   Q. Author Amy

___18. JANICE   R. Lindo's village

___19. SHOSHANA   S. ___ Directions

___20. BIBLE   T. Waverly's daughter

___21. FAITH   U. Rose defines it as an illusion that one is somehow in control.

___22. SUN   V. Moon Lady's husband lives there.

___23. ARCHITECT   W. Having no respect for ancestors or family

___24. WUTSING   X. Waverly's mother

___25. RICH   Y. He owned house where An-mei and her mother lived.

Copyrighted

Joy Luck Club Matching 1 Answer Key

I - 1. BLOOD
X - 2. LINDO
Q - 3. TAN
E - 4. HSU
K - 5. LEFTOVERS
W - 6. SHOU
N - 7. TURTLE
M - 8. CHINA
O - 9. PIANO
P - 10. SHANGHAI
S - 11. FOUR
F - 12. TAO
G - 13. MOON
J - 14. KWEILIN
R - 15. TAIYUAN
D - 16. LENA
B - 17. SOUP
C - 18. JANICE
T - 19. SHOSHANA
A - 20. BIBLE
U - 21. FAITH
V - 22. SUN
L - 23. ARCHITECT
Y - 24. WUTSING
H - 25. RICH

A. It is under the table leg in the kitchen.
B. It burned An-mei the night her mother returned.
C. Rose's sister
D. Ying-ying's daughter
E. An-mei ___; Rose ___ Jordan
F. This society gave Waverly her second chess set.
G. ___ Lady
H. Mr. Shields
I. Ying-ying got it on her clothes.
J. Original setting for JLC meetings
K. Meaning of 'yu' in Tyan-yu's name
L. Lena's profession
M. Waverly wants to go there for her second honeymoon.
N. It ate the tears.
O. Instrument Jing-mei played
P. Jing-mei goes there to find her sisters.
Q. Author Amy
R. Lindo's village
S. ___ Directions
T. Waverly's daughter
U. Rose defines it as an illusion that one is somehow in control.
V. Moon Lady's husband lives there.
W. Having no respect for ancestors or family
X. Waverly's mother
Y. He owned house where An-mei and her mother lived.

Copyrighted

Joy Luck Club Matching 2

___ 1. RING   A. He owned house where An-mei and her mother lived.

___ 2. GATES   B. He actually got the chess set for Christmas.

___ 3. TYANYU   C. The Twenty-six Malignant ___

___ 4. TREES   D. The eggs from the turtle's beak produced 7 of these.

___ 5. RULES   E. An-mei's name for her grandmother.

___ 6. COLD   F. Moon Lady became one.

___ 7. SHANGHAI   G. ___ Husband

___ 8. SHOUT   H. Lindo's husband via the matchmaker

___ 9. LINDO   I. Waverly's mother

___10. MAN   J. Ying-ying fell off the ___ and got separated from her family.

___11. BOAT   K. Instrument Jing-mei played

___12. POPO   L. Waiting Between The ___

___13. TED   M. Rose's husband

___14. VINCENT   N. Rose's mother threw her blue sapphire one into the water.

___15. PIANO   O. For An-mei to say her mother's name was to spit on her
                        father's ___.

___16. TAIYUAN   P. Jing-mei goes there to find her sisters.

___17. MAGPIES   Q. Ying-ying's wish was to be ___.

___18. BRIGHTNESS   R. Festival of Pure ___

___19. CANDLE   S. Necklace made of red jade

___20. GRAVE   T. It was supposed to be lit at both ends and kept burning all
                        night.

___21. TAITAI   U. On the third day after her mother died, An-mei learned to do
                        this.

___22. RICE   V. If the lips are gone, the teeth will be ___.

___23. WUTSING   W. Huang ___; Tyan-yu's mother

___24. FOUND   X. ___ of the Game

___25. CHANG   Y. Lindo's village

Copyrighted

N - 1. RING

A. He owned house where An-mei and her mother lived.

C - 2. GATES

B. He actually got the chess set for Christmas.

H - 3. TYANYU

C. The Twenty-six Malignant ___

L - 4. TREES

D. The eggs from the turtle's beak produced 7 of these.

X - 5. RULES

E. An-mei's name for her grandmother.

V - 6. COLD

F. Moon Lady became one.

P - 7. SHANGHAI

G. ___ Husband

U - 8. SHOUT

H. Lindo's husband via the matchmaker

I - 9. LINDO

I. Waverly's mother

F - 10. MAN

J. Ying-ying fell off the ___ and got separated from her family.

J - 11. BOAT

K. Instrument Jing-mei played

E - 12. POPO

L. Waiting Between The ___

M - 13. TED

M. Rose's husband

B - 14. VINCENT

N. Rose's mother threw her blue sapphire one into the water.

K - 15. PIANO

O. For An-mei to say her mother's name was to spit on her father's ___.

Y - 16. TAIYUAN

P. Jing-mei goes there to find her sisters.

D - 17. MAGPIES

Q. Ying-ying's wish was to be ___.

R - 18. BRIGHTNESS

R. Festival of Pure ___

T - 19. CANDLE

S. Necklace made of red jade

O - 20. GRAVE

T. It was supposed to be lit at both ends and kept burning all night.

W - 21. TAITAI

U. On the third day after her mother died, An-mei learned to do this.

G - 22. RICE

V. If the lips are gone, the teeth will be ___.

A - 23. WUTSING

W. Huang ___; Tyan-yu's mother

Q - 24. FOUND

X. ___ of the Game

S - 25. CHANG

Y. Lindo's village

Copyrighted

Joy Luck Club Matching 3

___ 1. GRAVE   A. It is under the table leg in the kitchen.

___ 2. SHOU   B. Ying-ying got it on her clothes.

___ 3. FRANCISCO   C. Ying-ying St. ___: Lena's mother

___ 4. LUCKY   D. An-mei and Lindo met at the ___ factory.

___ 5. POPO   E. An-mei ___; Rose ___ Jordan

___ 6. WOOD   F. An-mei's name for her grandmother.

___ 7. TAIYUAN   G. He actually got the chess set for Christmas.

___ 8. CHILD   H. Necklace made of red jade

___ 9. MOLE   I. Jong family lived there: San ___

___10. COOKIE   J. Moon Lady's husband lives there.

___11. VINCENT   K. For An-mei to say her mother's name was to spit on her father's ___.

___12. CHANG   L. The beads of An-mei's necklace from Second Wife were made of this.

___13. CLAIR   M. Waverly's daughter

___14. HSU   N. ___ Luck Club

___15. LENA   O. Ying-ying's daughter

___16. BLOOD   P. Having no respect for ancestors or family

___17. RULES   Q. Without ___

___18. GLASS   R. Proof of the rotting marriage

___19. SOUP   S. It burned An-mei the night her mother returned.

___20. SHOSHANA   T. The women hoped to be ___ and that was their only joy.

___21. JOY   U. ___ Face

___22. DOUBLE   V. 'Pleading ___'; Jing-mei's piano piece

___23. BING   W. Lindo's village

___24. BIBLE   X. He drowned.

___25. SUN   Y. ___ of the Game

Copyrighted

Joy Luck Club Matching 3 Answer Key

K - 1. GRAVE

A. It is under the table leg in the kitchen.

P - 2. SHOU

B. Ying-ying got it on her clothes.

I - 3. FRANCISCO

C. Ying-ying St. ___: Lena's mother

T - 4. LUCKY

D. An-mei and Lindo met at the ___ factory.

F - 5. POPO

E. An-mei ___; Rose ___ Jordan

Q - 6. WOOD

F. An-mei's name for her grandmother.

W - 7. TAIYUAN

G. He actually got the chess set for Christmas.

V - 8. CHILD

H. Necklace made of red jade

R - 9. MOLE

I. Jong family lived there: San ___

D -10. COOKIE

J. Moon Lady's husband lives there.

G -11. VINCENT

K. For An-mei to say her mother's name was to spit on her father's ___.

H -12. CHANG

L. The beads of An-mei's necklace from Second Wife were made of this.

C -13. CLAIR

M. Waverly's daughter

E -14. HSU

N. ___ Luck Club

O -15. LENA

O. Ying-ying's daughter

B -16. BLOOD

P. Having no respect for ancestors or family

Y -17. RULES

Q. Without ___

L -18. GLASS

R. Proof of the rotting marriage

S -19. SOUP

S. It burned An-mei the night her mother returned.

M -20. SHOSHANA

T. The women hoped to be ___ and that was their only joy.

N -21. JOY

U. ___ Face

U -22. DOUBLE

V. 'Pleading ___'; Jing-mei's piano piece

X -23. BING

W. Lindo's village

A -24. BIBLE

X. He drowned.

J - 25. SUN

Y. ___ of the Game

Copyrighted

Joy Luck Club Matching 4

___ 1. HEAVEN   A. Waverly's game

___ 2. MAGAZINES   B. Jing-mei's American name

___ 3. WUTSING   C. ___ Luck Club

___ 4. PIANO   D. Waverly's mother

___ 5. JOY   E. Best ___

___ 6. SUN   F. Moon Lady became one.

___ 7. SUYUAN   G. Where Ying-ying grew up

___ 8. SHOU   H. Jing-mei's mother: ___ Woo

___ 9. MAGPIES   I. 'Pleading ___'; Jing-mei's piano piece

___10. FOUND   J. Instrument Jing-mei played

___11. LIFESAVERS   K. He owned house where An-mei and her mother lived.

___12. JANICE   L. The eggs from the turtle's beak produced 7 of these.

___13. RICH   M. Lindo's husband via the matchmaker

___14. CHILD   N. Rose's sister

___15. MAN   O. Jong family hill: Three Steps to ___

___16. NINGPO   P. Moon Lady's husband lives there.

___17. TREES   Q. If the lips are gone, the teeth will be ___.

___18. SHOUT   R. Mr. Shields

___19. WUSHI   S. Ying-ying's wish was to be ___.

___20. LINDO   T. Where An-mei's family lived in China

___21. QUALITY   U. Waiting Between The ___

___22. TYANYU   V. Jing-mei's mother looked at these for stories about exceptional children.

___23. COLD   W. They took the place of the white knight and black pawn.

___24. JUNE   X. Having no respect for ancestors or family

___25. CHESS   Y. On the third day after her mother died, An-mei learned to do this.

Copyrighted

Joy Luck Club Matching 4 Answer Key

O - 1. HEAVEN   A. Waverly's game

V - 2. MAGAZINES   B. Jing-mei's American name

K - 3. WUTSING   C. ___ Luck Club

J - 4. PIANO   D. Waverly's mother

C - 5. JOY   E. Best ___

P - 6. SUN   F. Moon Lady became one.

H - 7. SUYUAN   G. Where Ying-ying grew up

X - 8. SHOU   H. Jing-mei's mother: ___ Woo

L - 9. MAGPIES   I. 'Pleading ___'; Jing-mei's piano piece

S -10. FOUND   J. Instrument Jing-mei played

W -11. LIFESAVERS   K. He owned house where An-mei and her mother lived.

N -12. JANICE   L. The eggs from the turtle's beak produced 7 of these.

R -13. RICH   M. Lindo's husband via the matchmaker

I - 14. CHILD   N. Rose's sister

F -15. MAN   O. Jong family hill: Three Steps to ___

T -16. NINGPO   P. Moon Lady's husband lives there.

U -17. TREES   Q. If the lips are gone, the teeth will be ___.

Y -18. SHOUT   R. Mr. Shields

G -19. WUSHI   S. Ying-ying's wish was to be ___.

D -20. LINDO   T. Where An-mei's family lived in China

E -21. QUALITY   U. Waiting Between The ___

M -22. TYANYU   V. Jing-mei's mother looked at these for stories about exceptional children.

Q -23. COLD   W. They took the place of the white knight and black pawn.

B -24. JUNE   X. Having no respect for ancestors or family

A -25. CHESS   Y. On the third day after her mother died, An-mei learned to do this.

Copyrighted

Joy Luck Club Magic Squares 1

Match the definition with the vocabulary word. Put your answers in the magic squares below. When your answers are correct, all columns and rows will add to the same number.

A. LENA   E. TAIYUAN   I. JEWELRY   M. YAN
B. CHANG   F. CANDLE   J. POPO   N. QUALITY
C. BIBLE   G. SUN   K. CHILD   O. SHANGHAI
D. MAN   H. TAN   L. BRIGHTNESS   P. NINGPO

1. Jing-mei goes there to find her sisters.
2. Moon Lady became one.
3. An-mei's name for her grandmother.
4. Lindo's village
5. Matchmaker suggested Lindo take off all her ___ to be better balanced.
6. It was supposed to be lit at both ends and kept burning all night.
7. Where An-mei's family lived in China
8. It is under the table leg in the kitchen.

9. Author Amy
10. 'Pleading ___'; Jing-mei's piano piece
11. Ying-ying's daughter
12. Best ___
13. Necklace made of red jade
14. An-mei's personal maid: ___ Chung
15. Moon Lady's husband lives there.
16. Festival of Pure ___

A=	B=	C=	D=
E=	F=	G=	H=
I=	J=	K=	L=
M=	N=	O=	P=

Copyrighted

Joy Luck Club Magic Squares 1 Answer Key

Match the definition with the vocabulary word. Put your answers in the magic squares below. When your answers are correct, all columns and rows will add to the same number.

A. LENA   E. TAIYUAN   I. JEWELRY   M. YAN
B. CHANG   F. CANDLE   J. POPO   N. QUALITY
C. BIBLE   G. SUN   K. CHILD   O. SHANGHAI
D. MAN   H. TAN   L. BRIGHTNESS   P. NINGPO

1. Jing-mei goes there to find her sisters.
2. Moon Lady became one.
3. An-mei's name for her grandmother.
4. Lindo's village
5. Matchmaker suggested Lindo take off all her ___ to be better balanced.
6. It was supposed to be lit at both ends and kept burning all night.
7. Where An-mei's family lived in China
8. It is under the table leg in the kitchen.

9. Author Amy
10. 'Pleading ___'; Jing-mei's piano piece
11. Ying-ying's daughter
12. Best ___
13. Necklace made of red jade
14. An-mei's personal maid: ___ Chung
15. Moon Lady's husband lives there.
16. Festival of Pure ___

A=11	B=13	C=8	D=2
E=4	F=6	G=15	H=9
I=5	J=3	K=10	L=16
M=14	N=12	O=1	P=7

Copyrighted

Joy Luck Club Magic Squares 2

Match the definition with the vocabulary word. Put your answers in the magic squares below. When your answers are correct, all columns and rows will add to the same number.

A. LAUPO	E. CRAB	I. CANDLE	M. FOUR
B. KINDS	F. VOICE	J. POPO	N. TAN
C. JOY	G. GLASS	K. LIFESAVERS	O. WAVERLY
D. TED	H. JUNE	L. MOON	P. JANICE

1. ___ Directions
2. ___ From the Wall
3. Jing-mei's American name
4. Lindo Jong's daughter
5. ___ Lady
6. ___ Luck Club
7. Waverly's neighbor who played chess with her
8. An-mei's name for her grandmother.
9. They took the place of the white knight and black pawn.
10. Rose's husband
11. Two ___
12. It was supposed to be lit at both ends and kept burning all night.
13. Author Amy
14. One with a lost leg on Chinese New Year is a bad sign.
15. The beads of An-mei's necklace from Second Wife were made of this.
16. Rose's sister

A=	B=	C=	D=
E=	F=	G=	H=
I=	J=	K=	L=
M=	N=	O=	P=

Copyrighted

Joy Luck Club Magic Squares 2 Answer Key

Match the definition with the vocabulary word. Put your answers in the magic squares below. When your answers are correct, all columns and rows will add to the same number.

A. LAUPO
B. KINDS
C. JOY
D. TED

E. CRAB
F. VOICE
G. GLASS
H. JUNE

I. CANDLE
J. POPO
K. LIFESAVERS
L. MOON

M. FOUR
N. TAN
O. WAVERLY
P. JANICE

1. ___ Directions
2. ___ From the Wall
3. Jing-mei's American name
4. Lindo Jong's daughter
5. ___ Lady
6. ___ Luck Club
7. Waverly's neighbor who played chess with her
8. An-mei's name for her grandmother.

9. They took the place of the white knight and black pawn.
10. Rose's husband
11. Two ___
12. It was supposed to be lit at both ends and kept burning all night.
13. Author Amy
14. One with a lost leg on Chinese New Year is a bad sign.
15. The beads of An-mei's necklace from Second Wife were made of this.
16. Rose's sister

A=7	B=11	C=6	D=10
E=14	F=2	G=15	H=3
I=12	J=8	K=9	L=5
M=1	N=13	O=4	P=16

Copyrighted

Joy Luck Club Magic Squares 3

Match the definition with the vocabulary word. Put your answers in the magic squares below. When your answers are correct, all columns and rows will add to the same number.

A. RICH
B. LIFESAVERS
C. TICKETS
D. TAO

E. YAN
F. MOON
G. MEIMEI
H. POPO

I. DOUBLE
J. TURTLE
K. MAGAZINES
L. LEFTOVERS

M. TAITAI
N. MAN
O. CHOU
P. TYANYU

1. An-mei's name for her grandmother.
2. Mr. Shields
3. They took the place of the white knight and black pawn.
4. Waverly's family called her this.
5. It ate the tears.
6. Sleep; visit Mr. ___
7. Lindo's husband via the matchmaker
8. ___ Face

9. Jing-mei's mother looked at these for stories about exceptional children.
10. Moon Lady became one.
11. Huang ___; Tyan-yu's mother
12. Meaning of 'yu' in Tyan-yu's name
13. An-mei's personal maid: ___ Chung
14. This society gave Waverly her second chess set.
15. A Pair Of ___
16. ___ Lady

A=	B=	C=	D=
E=	F=	G=	H=
I=	J=	K=	L=
M=	N=	O=	P=

Copyrighted

Joy Luck Club Magic Squares 3 Answer Key

Match the definition with the vocabulary word. Put your answers in the magic squares below. When your answers are correct, all columns and rows will add to the same number.

A. RICH
B. LIFESAVERS
C. TICKETS
D. TAO

E. YAN
F. MOON
G. MEIMEI
H. POPO

I. DOUBLE
J. TURTLE
K. MAGAZINES
L. LEFTOVERS

M. TAITAI
N. MAN
O. CHOU
P. TYANYU

1. An-mei's name for her grandmother.
2. Mr. Shields
3. They took the place of the white knight and black pawn.
4. Waverly's family called her this.
5. It ate the tears.
6. Sleep; visit Mr. ___
7. Lindo's husband via the matchmaker
8. ___ Face

9. Jing-mei's mother looked at these for stories about exceptional children.
10. Moon Lady became one.
11. Huang ___; Tyan-yu's mother
12. Meaning of 'yu' in Tyan-yu's name
13. An-mei's personal maid: ___ Chung
14. This society gave Waverly her second chess set.
15. A Pair Of ___
16. ___ Lady

A=2	B=3	C=15	D=14
E=13	F=16	G=4	H=1
I=8	J=5	K=9	L=12
M=11	N=10	O=6	P=7

Copyrighted

Joy Luck Club Magic Squares 4

Match the definition with the vocabulary word. Put your answers in the magic squares below. When your answers are correct, all columns and rows will add to the same number.

A. CLAIR   E. DOUBLE   I. TYANYU   M. ARCHITECT
B. GATES   F. COLD   J. SHANGHAI   N. TAITAI
C. BLOOD   G. BOAT   K. GRAVE   O. WAVERLY
D. MEIMEI   H. WOOD   L. QUALITY   P. TED

1. Ying-ying got it on her clothes.
2. Jing-mei goes there to find her sisters.
3. If the lips are gone, the teeth will be ___.
4. Lindo Jong's daughter
5. Rose's husband
6. ___ Face
7. Lindo's husband via the matchmaker
8. Waverly's family called her this.
9. Lena's profession
10. Without ___
11. Best ___
12. Ying-ying St. ___: Lena's mother
13. The Twenty-six Malignant ___
14. For An-mei to say her mother's name was to spit on her father's ___.
15. Ying-ying fell off the ___ and got separated from her family.
16. Huang ___; Tyan-yu's mother

A=	B=	C=	D=
E=	F=	G=	H=
I=	J=	K=	L=
M=	N=	O=	P=

Copyrighted

Joy Luck Club Magic Squares 4 Answer Key

Match the definition with the vocabulary word. Put your answers in the magic squares below. When your answers are correct, all columns and rows will add to the same number.

A. CLAIR
B. GATES
C. BLOOD
D. MEIMEI

E. DOUBLE
F. COLD
G. BOAT
H. WOOD

I. TYANYU
J. SHANGHAI
K. GRAVE
L. QUALITY

M. ARCHITECT
N. TAITAI
O. WAVERLY
P. TED

1. Ying-ying got it on her clothes.
2. Jing-mei goes there to find her sisters.
3. If the lips are gone, the teeth will be ___.
4. Lindo Jong's daughter
5. Rose's husband
6. ___ Face
7. Lindo's husband via the matchmaker
8. Waverly's family called her this.

9. Lena's profession
10. Without ___
11. Best ___
12. Ying-ying St. ___: Lena's mother
13. The Twenty-six Malignant ___
14. For An-mei to say her mother's name was to spit on her father's ___.
15. Ying-ying fell off the ___ and got separated from her family.
16. Huang ___; Tyan-yu's mother

A=12	B=13	C=1	D=8
E=6	F=3	G=15	H=10
I=7	J=2	K=14	L=11
M=9	N=16	O=4	P=5

Copyrighted

```
C H E S S H A N G H A I Z D U K X
H Z X S U O G E T F M C O O B Z J
U B A D Y P Z V A O Y O H R N E F
N L L U I T A I U W C I M W C V
G O F O A U I E Y N T G R E O I B
C D P N N M C H U D H S L G N O M
F N C R W F K W A T B R V C Z V N
S I R A E N E N N H Y L E T Q R K
U L A S H T E I A S N O A U T V
N N B I N G S E E R T S H O U P F
H I B O R S M U U O I B F O D C K
B R L A A I W L F L J C H C L G O
T C V E E T E R A D M S H A T N Z
P E N M N S D N I K T A I T A I Z
D Q D P U A A G T C N R N I N Z D
R E D X J Y O J H G E T P U O S Z
```

A Pair Of ___ (7)
An-mei ___; Rose ___ Jordan (3)
An-mei's personal maid: ___ Chung (3)
Author Amy (3)
Color of the candle (3)
Festival of Pure ___ (10)
For An-mei to say her mother's name was to spit
  on her father's ___. (5)
Having no respect for ancestors or family (4)
He actually got the chess set for Christmas. (7)
He drowned. (4)
He tormented Lena. (6)
Huang ___; Tyan-yu's mother (6)
If the lips are gone, the teeth will be ___. (4)
Instrument Jing-mei played (5)
It burned An-mei the night her mother returned. (4)
It is under the table leg in the kitchen. (5)
Jing-mei goes there to find her sisters. (8)
Jing-mei's American name (4)
Jing-mei's mother: ___ Woo (6)
Jong family hill: Three Steps to ___ (6)
Lena's husband (6)
Lindo taught Waverly the ___ of invisible strength.
  (3)
Lindo's village (7)
Matchmaker suggested Lindo take off all her ___
  to be better balanced. (7)
Moon Lady became one. (3)
Moon Lady's husband lives there. (3)
Mr. Shields (4)
Necklace made of red jade (5)
On the third day after her mother died, An-mei

learned to do this. (5)
One with a lost leg on Chinese New Year is a bad
  sign. (4)
Piano teacher (5)
Rose defines it as an illusion that one is somehow
  in control. (5)
Rose's husband (3)
Sleep; visit Mr. ___ (4)
Substance First Wife used (5)
The beads of An-mei's necklace from Second Wife
  were made of this. (5)
This society gave Waverly her second chess set.
  (3)
Two ___ (5)
Waiting Between The ___ (5)
Waverly's family called her this. (6)
Waverly's game (5)
Waverly's mother (5)
Without ___ (4)
Ying-ying St. ___: Lena's mother (5)
Ying-ying fell off the ___ and got separated from
  her family. (4)
Ying-ying got it on her clothes. (5)
Ying-ying's daughter (4)
Ying-ying's wish was to be ___. (5)
___ Directions (4)
___ From the Wall (5)
___ Husband (4)
___ Lady (4)
___ Luck Club (3)
___ of the Game (5)

Copyrighted

A Pair Of ___ (7)

An-mei ___; Rose ___ Jordan (3)

An-mei's personal maid: ___ Chung (3)

Author Amy (3)

Color of the candle (3)

Festival of Pure ___ (10)

For An-mei to say her mother's name was to spit on her father's ___. (5)

Having no respect for ancestors or family (4)

He actually got the chess set for Christmas. (7)

He drowned. (4)

He tormented Lena. (6)

Huang ___; Tyan-yu's mother (6)

If the lips are gone, the teeth will be ___. (4)

Instrument Jing-mei played (5)

It burned An-mei the night her mother returned. (4)

It is under the table leg in the kitchen. (5)

Jing-mei goes there to find her sisters. (8)

Jing-mei's American name (4)

Jing-mei's mother: ___ Woo (6)

Jong family hill: Three Steps to ___ (6)

Lena's husband (6)

Lindo taught Waverly the ___ of invisible strength. (3)

Lindo's village (7)

Matchmaker suggested Lindo take off all her ___ to be better balanced. (7)

Moon Lady became one. (3)

Moon Lady's husband lives there. (3)

Mr. Shields (4)

Necklace made of red jade (5)

On the third day after her mother died, An-mei learned to do this. (5)

One with a lost leg on Chinese New Year is a bad sign. (4)

Piano teacher (5)

Rose defines it as an illusion that one is somehow in control. (5)

Rose's husband (3)

Sleep; visit Mr. ___ (4)

Substance First Wife used (5)

The beads of An-mei's necklace from Second Wife were made of this. (5)

This society gave Waverly her second chess set. (3)

Two ___ (5)

Waiting Between The ___ (5)

Waverly's family called her this. (6)

Waverly's game (5)

Waverly's mother (5)

Without ___ (4)

Ying-ying St. ___: Lena's mother (5)

Ying-ying fell off the ___ and got separated from her family. (4)

Ying-ying got it on her clothes. (5)

Ying-ying's daughter (4)

Ying-ying's wish was to be ___. (5)

___ Directions (4)

___ From the Wall (5)

___ Husband (4)

___ Lady (4)

___ Luck Club (3)

___ of the Game (5)

Copyrighted

```
B  R  I  G  H  T  N  E  S  S  B  L  O  O  D  J  T
P  I  A  N  O  S  R  E  V  A  S  E  F  I  L  A  C
L  T  U  R  T  L  E  V  Z  N  I  N  G  P  O  N  E
W  X  D  M  F  A  I  T  H  Q  S  T  E  K  C  I  T
T  A  I  T  A  I  G  A  T  E  S  W  H  S  U  C  I
A  M  F  W  X  G  Z  H  R  C  A  N  D  L  E  E  H
Y  R  O  R  U  T  A  O  B  W  G  L  A  S  S  L  C
Q  L  T  L  A  S  B  Z  H  P  R  U  L  E  S  A  R
B  I  B  L  E  N  H  C  I  R  S  H  O  U  T  U  A
O  P  I  U  M  D  C  I  W  N  N  C  R  A  B  P  L
W  A  V  E  R  L  Y  I  K  W  E  I  L  I  N  O  I
C  I  A  H  G  N  A  H  S  P  C  S  Y  T  R  S  N
H  M  R  I  C  E  L  S  L  C  I  M  A  N  E  L  D
I  G  N  U  H  C  H  T  M  J  O  Y  N  E  D  D  O
L  E  I  K  O  O  C  X  A  O  V  F  R  I  A  L  C
D  Q  S  O  U  P  T  A  N  O  T  T  Y  A  N  Y  U
```

'Pleading ___'; Jing-mei's piano piece (5)

A Pair Of ___ (7)

An-mei ___; Rose ___ Jordan (3)

An-mei and Lindo met at the ___ factory. (6)

An-mei's personal maid: ___ Chung (3)

Author Amy (3)

Color of the candle (3)

Festival of Pure ___ (10)

Having no respect for ancestors or family (4)

Huang ___; Tyan-yu's mother (6)

If the lips are gone, the teeth will be ___. (4)

Instrument Jing-mei played (5)

It ate the tears. (6)

It burned An-mei the night her mother returned. (4)

It is under the table leg in the kitchen. (5)

It was supposed to be lit at both ends and kept burning all night. (6)

Jing-mei goes there to find her sisters. (8)

Jing-mei's mother looked at these for stories about exceptional children. (9)

Jong family lived there: San ___ (9)

Lena's profession (9)

Lindo Jong's daughter (7)

Lindo taught Waverly the ___ of invisible strength. (3)

Lindo's husband via the matchmaker (6)

Moon Lady became one. (3)

Mr. Shields (4)

On the third day after her mother died, An-mei learned to do this. (5)

One with a lost leg on Chinese New Year is a bad sign. (4)

Original setting for JLC meetings (7)

Piano teacher (5)

Proof of the rotting marriage (4)

Rose defines it as an illusion that one is somehow in control. (5)

Rose's husband (3)

Rose's sister (6)

Sleep; visit Mr. ___ (4)

Substance First Wife used (5)

The Twenty-six Malignant ___ (5)

The beads of An-mei's necklace from Second Wife were made of this. (5)

They took the place of the white knight and black pawn. (10)

This society gave Waverly her second chess set. (3)

Waiting Between The ___ (5)

Waverly's mother (5)

Waverly's neighbor who played chess with her (5)

Where An-mei's family lived in China (6)

Where Ying-ying grew up (5)

Ying-ying St. ___: Lena's mother (5)

Ying-ying fell off the ___ and got separated from her family. (4)

Ying-ying got it on her clothes. (5)

Ying-ying's daughter (4)

___ From the Wall (5)

___ Husband (4)

___ Lady (4)

___ Luck Club (3)

___ of the Game (5)

Copyrighted

Joy Luck Club Word Search 2 Answer Key

```
B  R  I  G  H  T  N  E  S  S  B  L  O  O  D  J  T
P  I  A  N  O  S  R  E  V  A  S  E  F  I  L  A  C
   T  U  R  T  L  E        N  I  N  G  P  O  N  E
      M  F  A  I  T  H     S  T  E  K  C  I  T
T  A  I  T  A  I  G  A  T  E  S     H  S  U  C  I
   R  O  R  U  T  A  O  B     G  A  N  D  L  E  E  H
      T  L  A  S  Z        G  L  A  S  S  L  C
B  I  B  L  E  N  H  C  I  R  R  U  L  E  S  A  R
O  P  I  U  M        C  I     N     C  R  A  B  P  L
W  A  V  E  R  L  Y  I  K  W  E  I  L  I  N  O  I
C  I  A  H  G  N  A  H  S     C  S  Y  T  R  S  N
H     R  I  C  E     S     C  I  M  A  N  E  L  D
I     G  N  U  H  C  H  T  M  J  O  Y  N  E  D  D  O
L     E  I  K  O  O  C     A  O  V     R  I  A  L  C
D     S  O  U  P  T  A  N  O        T  Y  A  N  Y  U
```

'Pleading ___'; Jing-mei's piano piece (5)
A Pair Of ___ (7)
An-mei ___; Rose ___ Jordan (3)
An-mei and Lindo met at the ___ factory. (6)
An-mei's personal maid: ___ Chung (3)
Author Amy (3)
Color of the candle (3)
Festival of Pure ___ (10)
Having no respect for ancestors or family (4)
Huang ___; Tyan-yu's mother (6)
If the lips are gone, the teeth will be ___. (4)
Instrument Jing-mei played (5)
It ate the tears. (6)
It burned An-mei the night her mother returned. (4)
It is under the table leg in the kitchen. (5)
It was supposed to be lit at both ends and kept
  burning all night. (6)
Jing-mei goes there to find her sisters. (8)
Jing-mei's mother looked at these for stories about
  exceptional children. (9)
Jong family lived there: San ___ (9)
Lena's profession (9)
Lindo Jong's daughter (7)
Lindo taught Waverly the ___ of invisible strength.
  (3)
Lindo's husband via the matchmaker (6)
Moon Lady became one. (3)
Mr. Shields (4)
On the third day after her mother died, An-mei
  learned to do this. (5)
One with a lost leg on Chinese New Year is a bad
  sign. (4)

Original setting for JLC meetings (7)
Piano teacher (5)
Proof of the rotting marriage (4)
Rose defines it as an illusion that one is somehow
  in control. (5)
Rose's husband (3)
Rose's sister (6)
Sleep; visit Mr. ___ (4)
Substance First Wife used (5)
The Twenty-six Malignant ___ (5)
The beads of An-mei's necklace from Second Wife
  were made of this. (5)
They took the place of the white knight and black
  pawn. (10)
This society gave Waverly her second chess set.
  (3)
Waiting Between The ___ (5)
Waverly's mother (5)
Waverly's neighbor who played chess with her (5)
Where An-mei's family lived in China (6)
Where Ying-ying grew up (5)
Ying-ying St. ___: Lena's mother (5)
Ying-ying fell off the ___ and got separated from
  her family. (4)
Ying-ying got it on her clothes. (5)
Ying-ying's daughter (4)
___ From the Wall (5)
___ Husband (4)
___ Lady (4)
___ Luck Club (3)
___ of the Game (5)

Copyrighted

```
R L M M F S H A N G H A I J T L T R A L
B U Q O P A N X N L R K R U E A A N P Z
F C L N O E I A G N L V O C O W I U G D N
C K R E L N H T O P G H N B H H E T P N O
A Y I A S C M L H X S A K D C I B L A R I
N T C N B Q D C X T U W T J S J T E K Y
D I H A D L D K R Y F W A E F C U E K Y
L C O N M S G D U F G N I R S R O X C Z
E K U A E N S S R U I P B Y T F S L P T
X E L H I V R A Y C G I L L F S E H D X
Z T M S M N N E A B G E H E L I Y P Y
J S T O E C A R M L K K F N V V K U A J
W U S H I Y L R E V A W T A O T O N C B
W N N S T T P P I D J H O R R S O I V W
G F C E T I W G L C G M V O E Y C N C C
R O R I A L C P L I E A E B D E N G J E
A U P N I A H K R A N N R I L A S P O B
V R O I Y U U B R H S D S N T O R O Y F
E L O M U Q N C H E S O G P L O I D B
C H X X A M G L S K C U M O T N N D C R
S H O U N C H I L D E T P F O U N D Z H
```

ARCHITECT	CLAIR	JUNE	POPO	TAIYUAN
ARNOLD	COLD	KINDS	QUALITY	TAN
ART	COOKIE	LAUPO	RED	TAO
BIBLE	CRAB	LEFTOVERS	RICE	TED
BING	FAITH	LENA	RICH	TICKETS
BLOOD	FOUND	LINDO	RING	TREES
BOAT	FOUR	LUCKY	RULES	TURTLE
BRIGHTNESS	FRANCISCO	MAGPIES	SHANGHAI	TYANYU
CANDLE	GATES	MAN	SHOSHANA	VOICE
CHANG	GLASS	MEIMEI	SHOU	WAVERLY
CHESS	GRAVE	MOLE	SHOUT	WOOD
CHILD	HSU	MOON	SOUP	WUSHI
CHINA	JANICE	NINGPO	SUN	WUTSING
CHOU	JEWELRY	OPIUM	SUYUAN	YAN
CHUNG	JOY	PIANO	TAITAI	

Copyrighted

```
R  L  M     F  S  H  A  N  G  H  A  I     J  T  L  T  R  A
   U     O     A  N     N     R        R  U  E  A  A  N
C  L  O  E  I     N  N           O  C  O  W  I  U
C  K  R  E  L  N  H  T  O     G  H  N  B  H  H  E  T  P
A  Y  I  A  S  C     L  H     S  A     C  I  T  T  R  I
N  T  C  N  B     D        U        T  J  S     T  T  R  I
D  I  H  A  D           Y        A  E     C  U  E     Y
L  C  O  U  M  S  G        U  F  G  N  I  R  S  R  O     C
E  K  U  A  E  N     S  R  U  I  P  B     T     S  L     T
   T     H  I     A  Y  C  G  I  L  L     S     E     D
   E     S  M     N  N  E  A  B     E     E        P  Y
J  S  T  O  E  C  A  R  M  L     F  N     V  K  U  A
W  U  S  H  I  Y  L  R  E  V  A  W  T  A  O     O  N
W  N  N  S  T  T  P     I  D     H  O  R     S  O  I  N
G  F  C  E  T  I     G  L  C  G  M  V  O  E     C  N  C
R  O  R  I  A  L  C     L  I  E  A  E  B  D  E  N  G  J  E
A  U  P  N  I  A  H     R  A  N  N  R  I  L  A  S  P  O  Y
V  R  O  I  Y  U  U  B     H  S  D  S  N  T  O  R  O  Y
E  L  O  M  U  Q  N  G  C  H  E  S  S  O  G  P     O  I  D  C
         A     M  G              U           O        D  C
S  H  O  U  N  C  H  I  L  D  E  T  P  F  O  U  N  D        H
```

ARCHITECT	CLAIR	JUNE	POPO	TAIYUAN
ARNOLD	COLD	KINDS	QUALITY	TAN
ART	COOKIE	LAUPO	RED	TAO
BIBLE	CRAB	LEFTOVERS	RICE	TED
BING	FAITH	LENA	RICH	TICKETS
BLOOD	FOUND	LINDO	RING	TREES
BOAT	FOUR	LUCKY	RULES	TURTLE
BRIGHTNESS	FRANCISCO	MAGPIES	SHANGHAI	TYANYU
CANDLE	GATES	MAN	SHOSHANA	VOICE
CHANG	GLASS	MEIMEI	SHOU	WAVERLY
CHESS	GRAVE	MOLE	SHOUT	WOOD
CHILD	HSU	MOON	SOUP	WUSHI
CHINA	JANICE	NINGPO	SUN	WUTSING
CHOU	JEWELRY	OPIUM	SUYUAN	YAN
CHUNG	JOY	PIANO	TAITAI	

Copyrighted

```
R C H U N G G G C T M J E W E L R Y R Y
U T T V T W A R H Y D E E L B I B W K Z
L U A O V A T A I A M M I K T D V C M J
E R I I I V E V L N K A K M R A U X M H
S T Y C N E S E D Y M G O M E L I Y A M
R L U E R X J D U P P O N M I H T G G C
I E A J E L B U C K O I C M O R J I A C
N W N K N Y R N W H P E B A O A T L Z I
G N I S T U W E P U O S H A N G H A I Y
L B B R H A I B D P S U U I L D N U N D
I I A H K L O D U A O P C N Y A L Q E W
F N R D I S D A L L P E X O H Z Q E S A
E G C N D R L G N Y I Y J S F M A N R S
S T H N O I O N I A U N O Q O K F N I B
A R I T U C R A N N M H D L U C O B C K
V K N I B H A H G P S C E O N L U L E L
E N A C L S H C P P I N H H D O R O R H
R H W K E H H B O K A A C E H D D O C L
S G O E K O H F O D B B N S S L T D P J
H N O T W U S H I A W Q J O O S E E R T
Z Q D S Q T U F A I T H S C L A I R D S
```

ARNOLD	COOKIE	KINDS	PIANO	TAIYUAN
ART	CRAB	KWEILIN	POPO	TAN
BIBLE	DOUBLE	LAUPO	QUALITY	TAO
BING	FAITH	LENA	RED	TED
BLOOD	FOUND	LIFESAVERS	RICE	TICKETS
BOAT	FOUR	LINDO	RICH	TREES
CANDLE	GATES	LUCKY	RING	TURTLE
CHANG	GLASS	MAGAZINES	RULES	TYANYU
CHESS	GRAVE	MAGPIES	SHANGHAI	VINCENT
CHILD	HAROLD	MAN	SHOSHANA	VOICE
CHINA	HSU	MEIMEI	SHOU	WAVERLY
CHOU	JANICE	MOLE	SHOUT	WOOD
CHUNG	JEWELRY	MOON	SOUP	WUSHI
CLAIR	JOY	NINGPO	SUN	WUTSING
COLD	JUNE	OPIUM	TAITAI	YAN

```
R  C  H  U  N  G  G  G  C  T     M  J  E  W  E  L  R  Y        Y
U  T  T  V     W  A  R  H  Y        E  E  L  B  I  B           K
L  U  A  O  V  A  T  A  I  N        M  I     T        C
E  R  I  I  I  T  E  V  L  Y        A  K  M     A  U           M
S  T  Y  C  N  E  S  E  D  U     P  P  O  O     M  E  L  I  T  A  G
R  L  U  E     R  L  J     U  C  K  O  O        M     J  I  L  A  G
I     E  A     E  Y  R  N  N     H  P  E     A  O  A  T  L  A  Z  I
N     N     N  N  W  E  P  U  O  P  O  S  H  A  N  G  H  A  I
G  N     S  T  U  W  E  P  D  P  S  U  U  I        D  N  U  N  E
L  I  B  B  R  A  I     U  U  A  P  S  C  N  Y  A  L  Q  E  S
I  I  N  R     L  O     U  A  L  P  O  E     O  H     E  S  A
F  E  B  R  I  S  D  R  G  N  Y  A  I     J  S  F  M  A  N  R
E  S  C  N  D  R  L  O  N  I  A  U  N  O  U  O     F  N  B  I
S  H  I  T  O  U  C  R  A  N  N  M  H  D  L  U     O  B  L  C
A  I  N  I  B  H  A  H  G  P  S  C  E  O  N  L  U  R  O  E
V  K  A  N  U  S  H  C  P  B  O  I  N  H     D  R  O
E     W  I  L  E     H  P  O     A  A  N  E  H     D  O
R     O  C  E  O  H     B  O     A  A     N  S  S  L  T  D
S     O  K     O  H        O           O  O  S  E  E  R  T
      O  E  W  U  S  H  I  A                 O     S  E     R  T
      D  T  S     T  U  F  A  I  T  H        C  L  A  I  R  D
```

ARNOLD	COOKIE	KINDS	PIANO	TAIYUAN
ART	CRAB	KWEILIN	POPO	TAN
BIBLE	DOUBLE	LAUPO	QUALITY	TAO
BING	FAITH	LENA	RED	TED
BLOOD	FOUND	LIFESAVERS	RICE	TICKETS
BOAT	FOUR	LINDO	RICH	TREES
CANDLE	GATES	LUCKY	RING	TURTLE
CHANG	GLASS	MAGAZINES	RULES	TYANYU
CHESS	GRAVE	MAGPIES	SHANGHAI	VINCENT
CHILD	HAROLD	MAN	SHOSHANA	VOICE
CHINA	HSU	MEIMEI	SHOU	WAVERLY
CHOU	JANICE	MOLE	SHOUT	WOOD
CHUNG	JEWELRY	MOON	SOUP	WUSHI
CLAIR	JOY	NINGPO	SUN	WUTSING
COLD	JUNE	OPIUM	TAITAI	YAN

Copyrighted

Joy Luck Club Crossword 1

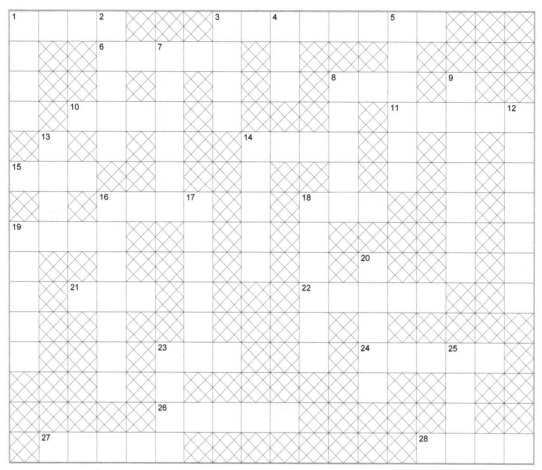

Across

1. One with a lost leg on Chinese New Year is a bad sign.
3. Jing-mei goes there to find her sisters.
6. Waverly's mother
8. Author Amy
10. ___ Lady
11. Substance First Wife used
14. ___ Husband
15. ___ Luck Club
16. Without ___
18. An-mei ___; Rose ___ Jordan
19. Ying-ying's daughter
21. Rose's husband
22. ___ From the Wall
23. Color of the candle
24. Waverly's neighbor who played chess with her
26. Piano teacher
27. Rose defines it as an illusion that one is somehow in control.
28. Ying-ying fell off the ___ and got separated from her family.

Down

1. Sleep; visit Mr. ___
2. Ying-ying got it on her clothes.
3. It burned An-mei the night her mother returned.
4. Lindo taught Waverly the ___ of invisible strength.
5. He tormented Lena.
7. Where An-mei's family lived in China
8. Waiting Between The ___
9. A Pair Of ___
12. The eggs from the turtle's beak produced 7 of these.
13. Proof of the rotting marriage
14. ___ of the Game
16. Lindo Jong's daughter
17. ___ Face
18. Jong family hill: Three Steps to ___
19. The women hoped to be ___ and that was their only joy.
20. It is under the table leg in the kitchen.
23. Mr. Shields
25. An-mei's name for her grandmother.

.

Copyrighted

1 C	R	A	**2** B			**3** S	H	**4** A	N	G	H	**5** A	I	
H			**6** L	I	**7** N	D	O		R			R	
O			O		I		U		T		**8** T	A	N		**9** T
U		**10** M	O	O	N		P			R		**11** O	P	I	U	**12** M
	13 M		D		G			**14** R	I	C	E		L		C	A
15 J	O	Y			P			U			E		D		K	G
	L		**16** W	O	O	**17** D		L		**18** H	S	U		E		P
19 L	E	N	A			O		E		E			T		I
U			V			U		S		A		**20** B		S		E
C		**21** T	E	D		B			**22** V	O	I	C	E		S
K			R			L			E		B			
Y			L		**23** R	E	D		N		**24** L	A	U	**25** P	O
			Y		I						E			O	
				26 C	H	U	N	G					P	
	27 F	A	I	T	H						**28** B	O	A	T

Across

1. One with a lost leg on Chinese New Year is a bad sign.
3. Jing-mei goes there to find her sisters.
6. Waverly's mother
8. Author Amy
10. ___ Lady
11. Substance First Wife used
14. ___ Husband
15. ___ Luck Club
16. Without ___
18. An-mei ___; Rose ___ Jordan
19. Ying-ying's daughter
21. Rose's husband
22. ___ From the Wall
23. Color of the candle
24. Waverly's neighbor who played chess with her
26. Piano teacher
27. Rose defines it as an illusion that one is somehow in control.
28. Ying-ying fell off the ___ and got separated from her family.

Down

1. Sleep; visit Mr. ___
2. Ying-ying got it on her clothes.
3. It burned An-mei the night her mother returned.
4. Lindo taught Waverly the ___ of invisible strength.
5. He tormented Lena.
7. Where An-mei's family lived in China
8. Waiting Between The ___
9. A Pair Of ___
12. The eggs from the turtle's beak produced 7 of these.
13. Proof of the rotting marriage
14. ___ of the Game
16. Lindo Jong's daughter
17. ___ Face
18. Jong family hill: Three Steps to ___
19. The women hoped to be ___ and that was their only joy.
20. It is under the table leg in the kitchen.
23. Mr. Shields
25. An-mei's name for her grandmother.

Copyrighted

Joy Luck Club Crossword 2

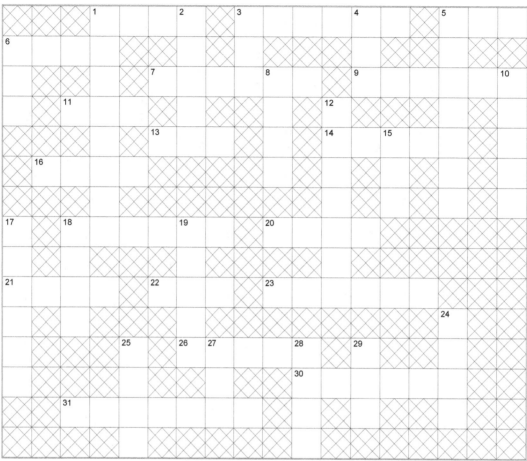

Across

1. It burned An-mei the night her mother returned.
3. Lindo's husband via the matchmaker
5. Moon Lady became one.
6. Mr. Shields
7. It was supposed to be lit at both ends and kept burning all night.
9. Where An-mei's family lived in China
11. An-mei ___; Rose ___ Jordan
13. ___ Luck Club
14. Where Ying-ying grew up
16. Ying-ying fell off the ___ and got separated from her family.
18. Rose's sister
20. If the lips are gone, the teeth will be ___.
21. Rose's mother threw her blue sapphire one into the water.
22. This society gave Waverly her second chess set.
23. He tormented Lena.
26. The Twenty-six Malignant ___
30. Jong family hill: Three Steps to ___
31. A Pair Of ___

.

Down

1. Waverly's daughter
2. Instrument Jing-mei played
3. Rose's husband
4. An-mei's personal maid: ___ Chung
5. The eggs from the turtle's beak produced 7 of these.
6. Color of the candle
8. Ying-ying's daughter
10. Substance First Wife used
12. Original setting for JLC meetings
15. Moon Lady's husband lives there.
17. It ate the tears.
18. Jing-mei's American name
19. Necklace made of red jade
24. He drowned.
25. ___ Husband
27. Lindo taught Waverly the ___ of invisible strength.
28. Having no respect for ancestors or family
29. Author Amy

Copyrighted

Joy Luck Club Crossword 2 Answer Key

		1			2		3				4			5		
		S	O	U	P		T	Y	A	N	Y	U		M	A	N
6 R	I	C	H			I		E			A			A		
E		O		7 C	A	N	D	8 L	E		9 N	I	N	G	P	10 O
D		11 H	S	U		N		E		12 K				P		P
		H		13 J	O	Y		N		14 W	U	15 S	H	I		I
16 B	O	A	T					A		E		U		E		U
		N								I		N		S		M
17 T	18 J	A	N	I	19 C	E		20 C	O	L	D					
U	U				H				I							
21 R	I	N	G		22 T	A	O		23 A	R	N	O	L	D		
T	E				A									24 B		
L		25 R		26 G	27 A	T	E	28 S	29 T					I		
E		I			R			30 H	E	A	V	E	N			
	31 T	I	C	K	E	T	S	O		N		G				
	E							U								

Across

1. It burned An-mei the night her mother returned.
3. Lindo's husband via the matchmaker
5. Moon Lady became one.
6. Mr. Shields
7. It was supposed to be lit at both ends and kept burning all night.
9. Where An-mei's family lived in China
11. An-mei ___; Rose ___ Jordan
13. ___ Luck Club
14. Where Ying-ying grew up
16. Ying-ying fell off the ___ and got separated from her family.
18. Rose's sister
20. If the lips are gone, the teeth will be ___.
21. Rose's mother threw her blue sapphire one into the water.
22. This society gave Waverly her second chess set.
23. He tormented Lena.
26. The Twenty-six Malignant ___
30. Jong family hill: Three Steps to ___
31. A Pair Of ___

Down

1. Waverly's daughter
2. Instrument Jing-mei played
3. Rose's husband
4. An-mei's personal maid: ___ Chung
5. The eggs from the turtle's beak produced 7 of these.
6. Color of the candle
8. Ying-ying's daughter
10. Substance First Wife used
12. Original setting for JLC meetings
15. Moon Lady's husband lives there.
17. It ate the tears.
18. Jing-mei's American name
19. Necklace made of red jade
24. He drowned.
25. ___ Husband
27. Lindo taught Waverly the ___ of invisible strength.
28. Having no respect for ancestors or family
29. Author Amy

41
Copyrighted

Joy Luck Club Crossword 3

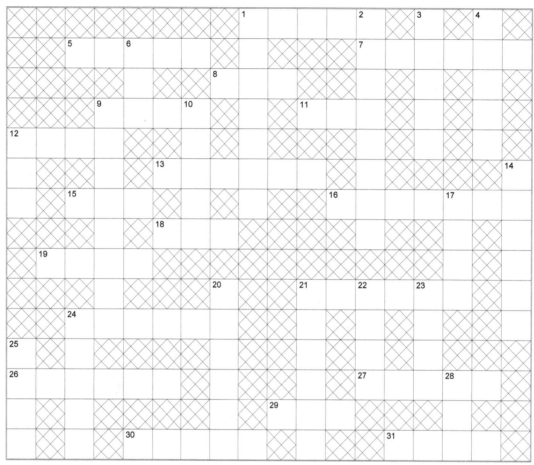

Across

1. Two ___
5. The Twenty-six Malignant ___
7. Lena's husband
8. Rose's husband
9. It burned An-mei the night her mother returned.
11. An-mei's personal maid: ___ Chung
12. Mr. Shields
13. Rose's sister
15. An-mei ___; Rose ___ Jordan
16. Lindo Jong's daughter
18. ___ Luck Club
19. Ying-ying fell off the ___ and got separated from her family.
21. It ate the tears.
24. It was supposed to be lit at both ends and kept burning all night.
26. Jong family hill: Three Steps to ___
27. The beads of An-mei's necklace from Second Wife were made of this.
29. Moon Lady became one.
30. Ying-ying St. ___: Lena's mother
31. Jing-mei's American name

Down

1. Original setting for JLC meetings
2. Jing-mei goes there to find her sisters.
3. Waiting Between The ___
4. Ying-ying got it on her clothes.
6. This society gave Waverly her second chess set.
9. Waverly's daughter
10. Instrument Jing-mei played
12. Color of the candle
14. Lindo's husband via the matchmaker
17. ___ Husband
20. Waverly's family called her this.
21. Huang ___; Tyan-yu's mother
22. Rose's mother threw her blue sapphire one into the water.
23. Ying-ying's daughter
24. Necklace made of red jade
25. Having no respect for ancestors or family
28. Moon Lady's husband lives there.

42
Copyrighted

							1 K	I	N	D	2 S		3 T		4 B	
		5 G	A	6 T	E	S		W			7 H	A	R	O	L	D
				A			8 T	E	D		A		E		O	
		9 S	O	U	10 P		I		11 Y	A	N		E		O	
12 R	I	C	H		I		L		G		S		D			
E			O	13 J	A	N	I	C	E		H				14 T	
D		15 H	S	U		N		N		16 W	A	V	E	17 R	L	Y
		H		18 J	O	Y				I				I		A
19 B	O	A	T										C		N	
	N			20 M		21 T	U	22 R	23 T	L	E		Y			
24 C	A	N	D	L	E		A		I		E		U			
25 S	H			I			I		N		N					
26 H	E	A	V	E	N		M		27 T	G	L	28 A	S	S		
O	N			E		29 M	A	N				U				
U	G	30 C	L	A	I	R		I		31 J	U	N	E			

Across
1. Two ___
5. The Twenty-six Malignant ___
7. Lena's husband
8. Rose's husband
9. It burned An-mei the night her mother returned.
11. An-mei's personal maid: ___ Chung
12. Mr. Shields
13. Rose's sister
15. An-mei ___; Rose ___ Jordan
16. Lindo Jong's daughter
18. ___ Luck Club
19. Ying-ying fell off the ___ and got separated from her family.
21. It ate the tears.
24. It was supposed to be lit at both ends and kept burning all night.
26. Jong family hill: Three Steps to ___
27. The beads of An-mei's necklace from Second Wife were made of this.
29. Moon Lady became one.
30. Ying-ying St. ___: Lena's mother
31. Jing-mei's American name

Down
1. Original setting for JLC meetings
2. Jing-mei goes there to find her sisters.
3. Waiting Between The ___
4. Ying-ying got it on her clothes.
6. This society gave Waverly her second chess set.
9. Waverly's daughter
10. Instrument Jing-mei played
12. Color of the candle
14. Lindo's husband via the matchmaker
17. ___ Husband
20. Waverly's family called her this.
21. Huang ___; Tyan-yu's mother
22. Rose's mother threw her blue sapphire one into the water.
23. Ying-ying's daughter
24. Necklace made of red jade
25. Having no respect for ancestors or family
28. Moon Lady's husband lives there.

Copyrighted

Joy Luck Club Crossword 4

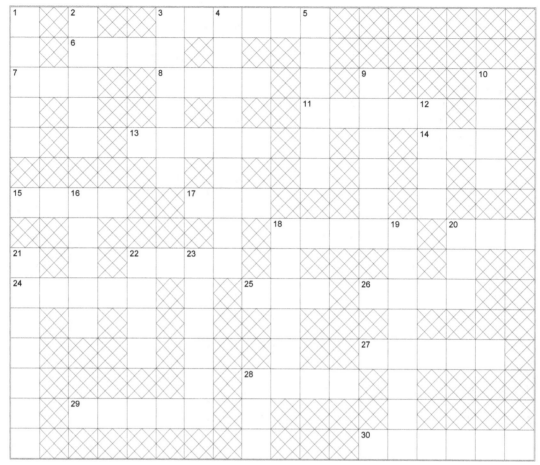

Across

3. Jong family hill: Three Steps to ___
6. Ying-ying's daughter
7. This society gave Waverly her second chess set.
8. ___ Husband
11. The beads of An-mei's necklace from Second Wife were made of this.
13. Ying-ying St. ___: Lena's mother
14. An-mei ___; Rose ___ Jordan
15. Mr. Shields
17. Color of the candle
18. Waiting Between The ___
20. Author Amy
22. Ying-ying fell off the ___ and got separated from her family.
24. Where Ying-ying grew up
25. An-mei's personal maid: ___ Chung
26. If the lips are gone, the teeth will be ___.
27. Necklace made of red jade
28. Jing-mei's American name
29. 'Pleading ___'; Jing-mei's piano piece
30. It was supposed to be lit at both ends and kept burning all night.

Down

1. The Twenty-six Malignant ___
2. Ying-ying got it on her clothes.
3. Lena's husband
4. Lena's profession
5. Where An-mei's family lived in China
9. Rose's sister
10. It burned An-mei the night her mother returned.
12. Having no respect for ancestors or family
16. Waverly's game
18. Lindo's husband via the matchmaker
19. Waverly's daughter
20. Rose's husband
21. Original setting for JLC meetings
22. He drowned.
23. He tormented Lena.
28. ___ Luck Club

Copyrighted

Joy Luck Club Crossword 4 Answer Key

1 G		2 B			3 H	E	4 A	V	E	5 N							
A		6 L	E	N	A		R			I							
7 T	A	O			8 R	I	C	E		N		9 J				10 S	
E		O			O		H			11 G	L	A	S	12 S		O	
S		D		13 C	L	A	I	R		P		N		14 H	S	U	
					D		T			O		I		O		P	
15 R	I	16 C	H			17 R	E	D				C		U			
		H					C		18 T	R	E	E	19 S		20 T	A	N
21 K		E		22 B	O	23 A	T		Y				H		E		
24 W	U	S	H	I		R		25 Y	A	N		26 C	O	L	D		
E		S		N		N			N				S				
I				G		O			Y			27 C	H	A	N	G	
L						L		28 J	U	N	E		A				
I		29 C	H	I	L	D		O					N				
N								Y				30 C	A	N	D	L	E

Across
3. Jong family hill: Three Steps to ___
6. Ying-ying's daughter
7. This society gave Waverly her second chess set.
8. ___ Husband
11. The beads of An-mei's necklace from Second Wife were made of this.
13. Ying-ying St. ___: Lena's mother
14. An-mei ___; Rose ___ Jordan
15. Mr. Shields
17. Color of the candle
18. Waiting Between The ___
20. Author Amy
22. Ying-ying fell off the ___ and got separated from her family.
24. Where Ying-ying grew up
25. An-mei's personal maid: ___ Chung
26. If the lips are gone, the teeth will be ___.
27. Necklace made of red jade
28. Jing-mei's American name
29. 'Pleading ___'; Jing-mei's piano piece
30. It was supposed to be lit at both ends and kept burning all night.

Down
1. The Twenty-six Malignant ___
2. Ying-ying got it on her clothes.
3. Lena's husband
4. Lena's profession
5. Where An-mei's family lived in China
9. Rose's sister
10. It burned An-mei the night her mother returned.
12. Having no respect for ancestors or family
16. Waverly's game
18. Lindo's husband via the matchmaker
19. Waverly's daughter
20. Rose's husband
21. Original setting for JLC meetings
22. He drowned.
23. He tormented Lena.
28. ___ Luck Club

Copyrighted

Joy Luck Club

MEIMEI	YAN	FRANCISCO	ARCHITECT	TAITAI
RICE	LINDO	CHUNG	CRAB	ARNOLD
TED	JOY	FREE SPACE	RICH	PIANO
CLAIR	WUSHI	TYANYU	OPIUM	HSU
FOUR	MAGPIES	SUN	FAITH	CHOU

Joy Luck Club

BRIGHTNESS	TREES	MAGAZINES	WAVERLY	WUTSING
COLD	BOAT	CANDLE	JEWELRY	COOKIE
HAROLD	GRAVE	FREE SPACE	KWEILIN	SHOSHANA
JANICE	VOICE	TICKETS	ART	RED
JUNE	POPO	RING	SHOU	WOOD

Copyrighted

Joy Luck Club

YAN	JUNE	RICH	TYANYU	SHOUT
SHANGHAI	QUALITY	GRAVE	KINDS	OPIUM
LIFESAVERS	FOUR	FREE SPACE	BRIGHTNESS	PIANO
HAROLD	SHOSHANA	VOICE	RICE	SUN
CRAB	BING	SOUP	SUYUAN	ARCHITECT

Joy Luck Club

JEWELRY	VINCENT	WOOD	MAGPIES	WUTSING
TAO	CHOU	TAN	MOON	BLOOD
COLD	FOUND	FREE SPACE	CLAIR	CHESS
LAUPO	KWEILIN	RING	FRANCISCO	TREES
GATES	WUSHI	CHILD	SHOU	CHINA

Copyrighted

Joy Luck Club

SHANGHAI	YAN	TICKETS	BING	MOLE
PIANO	RED	SOUP	VOICE	CHUNG
WUTSING	MAGPIES	FREE SPACE	LENA	HAROLD
RING	MEIMEI	JUNE	ARNOLD	FOUR
GLASS	NINGPO	WOOD	ART	BLOOD

Joy Luck Club

CHINA	GRAVE	FOUND	WUSHI	FRANCISCO
KINDS	RICH	ARCHITECT	LAUPO	LEFTOVERS
SUYUAN	WAVERLY	FREE SPACE	COOKIE	VINCENT
JANICE	CRAB	CANDLE	RULES	LIFESAVERS
HEAVEN	RICE	BOAT	SHOSHANA	TED

Copyrighted

Joy Luck Club

ARNOLD	CANDLE	BING	COOKIE	GRAVE
RICH	FOUR	LIFESAVERS	KWEILIN	TAN
LENA	RING	FREE SPACE	MOLE	KINDS
NINGPO	TYANYU	RED	BLOOD	MAN
CHANG	QUALITY	JOY	BIBLE	DOUBLE

Joy Luck Club

LUCKY	WUTSING	TED	POPO	VOICE
MOON	CHILD	ARCHITECT	GATES	BOAT
LINDO	SHOU	FREE SPACE	MEIMEI	YAN
SUN	LEFTOVERS	PIANO	FAITH	CHUNG
HEAVEN	RICE	MAGAZINES	TREES	MAGPIES

Copyrighted

Joy Luck Club

PIANO	MOON	VINCENT	MAGPIES	RING
BOAT	JOY	QUALITY	SHANGHAI	TYANYU
GLASS	GATES	FREE SPACE	RED	CHOU
BING	CHANG	KWEILIN	OPIUM	JUNE
WUTSING	BRIGHTNESS	TAO	SHOUT	CANDLE

Joy Luck Club

POPO	WAVERLY	LIFESAVERS	YAN	COOKIE
SHOU	TAN	LEFTOVERS	VOICE	WOOD
GRAVE	ARCHITECT	FREE SPACE	TAITAI	BLOOD
RICH	FOUR	MAGAZINES	MAN	RULES
FOUND	HEAVEN	MEIMEI	MOLE	CRAB

Copyrighted

Joy Luck Club

MOON	RULES	SHOU	LENA	CHESS
COLD	MEIMEI	CHANG	ARCHITECT	BOAT
HAROLD	SUYUAN	FREE SPACE	GLASS	BLOOD
MAN	CLAIR	JOY	BING	SUN
FRANCISCO	TAITAI	TAIYUAN	RICH	WAVERLY

Joy Luck Club

TURTLE	SHANGHAI	TYANYU	LAUPO	JANICE
BIBLE	TICKETS	CHOU	TAN	ARNOLD
LINDO	MAGPIES	FREE SPACE	CANDLE	YAN
POPO	WUTSING	SOUP	PIANO	OPIUM
ART	COOKIE	WOOD	LIFESAVERS	RED

Copyrighted

Joy Luck Club

BOAT	WUTSING	RED	CHESS	TED
BRIGHTNESS	BLOOD	CHINA	GLASS	TAO
MAGAZINES	HEAVEN	FREE SPACE	CLAIR	FOUND
NINGPO	VOICE	WOOD	CHANG	SOUP
LEFTOVERS	TAIYUAN	MAGPIES	SHOUT	TURTLE

Joy Luck Club

LAUPO	CHUNG	VINCENT	ARNOLD	TAITAI
SUN	BIBLE	KWEILIN	ARCHITECT	HAROLD
GATES	MOLE	FREE SPACE	ART	KINDS
RULES	SHOSHANA	CANDLE	YAN	LIFESAVERS
TYANYU	TICKETS	COLD	RING	MAN

Copyrighted

Joy Luck Club

TURTLE	CHESS	SUN	ARCHITECT	MAGAZINES
TICKETS	CHILD	FRANCISCO	SOUP	BOAT
RICE	TAITAI	FREE SPACE	CHINA	POPO
CRAB	QUALITY	ARNOLD	SUYUAN	TREES
MAGPIES	RED	DOUBLE	CHOU	LUCKY

Joy Luck Club

YAN	SHOSHANA	FAITH	MAN	SHANGHAI
TYANYU	SHOU	MOON	LINDO	GRAVE
HSU	FOUND	FREE SPACE	HEAVEN	WUTSING
LENA	LEFTOVERS	TAO	MEIMEI	CHANG
LAUPO	GLASS	MOLE	KWEILIN	KINDS

Copyrighted

Joy Luck Club

FAITH	LAUPO	MAGAZINES	JEWELRY	NINGPO
TAN	TAIYUAN	GATES	SHOUT	VOICE
QUALITY	RICH	FREE SPACE	FOUND	WAVERLY
CHUNG	SHOSHANA	MAN	DOUBLE	OPIUM
LENA	JOY	SUN	LIFESAVERS	BOAT

Joy Luck Club

COOKIE	PIANO	TREES	RING	WOOD
SOUP	ARNOLD	CRAB	GLASS	ART
TED	WUTSING	FREE SPACE	COLD	LINDO
BLOOD	GRAVE	BRIGHTNESS	MOLE	KWEILIN
SHANGHAI	CLAIR	TAO	BING	FOUR

Copyrighted

Joy Luck Club

SOUP	COLD	LAUPO	HSU	CHANG
TED	TREES	TAN	JUNE	CHILD
GATES	KINDS	FREE SPACE	QUALITY	RICE
BOAT	SHOSHANA	SHOU	TURTLE	CHUNG
LIFESAVERS	JOY	VINCENT	CHOU	WUSHI

Joy Luck Club

COOKIE	ARCHITECT	BIBLE	WUTSING	LINDO
SHANGHAI	PIANO	MOLE	POPO	RULES
HAROLD	TAO	FREE SPACE	FOUND	MAN
FAITH	BING	RING	ART	TAITAI
BRIGHTNESS	SUN	KWEILIN	DOUBLE	CHESS

Copyrighted

Joy Luck Club

SHANGHAI	HSU	GATES	MAGPIES	SOUP
KWEILIN	BOAT	RICE	TICKETS	BLOOD
LUCKY	SHOUT	FREE SPACE	CLAIR	LAUPO
ARNOLD	TAO	SUN	GRAVE	BRIGHTNESS
SHOU	LENA	CHOU	NINGPO	RING

Joy Luck Club

TAITAI	WAVERLY	PIANO	JANICE	CHUNG
WUTSING	WUSHI	SHOSHANA	MEIMEI	JOY
TYANYU	TREES	FREE SPACE	JUNE	FOUND
ART	LEFTOVERS	SUYUAN	RICH	VOICE
CHINA	CANDLE	TURTLE	CRAB	CHILD

Copyrighted

Joy Luck Club

CHUNG	SHANGHAI	VINCENT	ARCHITECT	POPO
TICKETS	MAN	WUTSING	NINGPO	JEWELRY
WOOD	SHOUT	FREE SPACE	LINDO	RICE
YAN	FAITH	GLASS	RICH	BRIGHTNESS
CLAIR	TURTLE	CHOU	CRAB	BIBLE

Joy Luck Club

JUNE	WAVERLY	FOUR	TED	VOICE
GRAVE	TAITAI	RULES	MOLE	SHOU
HEAVEN	GATES	FREE SPACE	FOUND	LEFTOVERS
ART	RING	MAGAZINES	CHILD	HSU
BLOOD	BOAT	ARNOLD	BING	QUALITY

Copyrighted

Joy Luck Club

JOY	COLD	BRIGHTNESS	LAUPO	TAIYUAN
SHOSHANA	CANDLE	WOOD	TREES	BLOOD
POPO	TURTLE	FREE SPACE	WUSHI	CLAIR
HEAVEN	BING	CHANG	MAGPIES	LINDO
TYANYU	CHESS	MAN	RICH	WAVERLY

Joy Luck Club

LUCKY	FAITH	JUNE	FOUR	CHILD
KWEILIN	TAITAI	TED	LENA	JEWELRY
TICKETS	GRAVE	FREE SPACE	CHUNG	MOON
HAROLD	TAN	CRAB	HSU	RED
ART	QUALITY	SHOUT	LEFTOVERS	MEIMEI

Copyrighted

Joy Luck Club

BOAT	RING	JEWELRY	JOY	BIBLE
JUNE	WAVERLY	WUSHI	BRIGHTNESS	POPO
LENA	CHANG	FREE SPACE	CHINA	LINDO
CHUNG	KINDS	RICH	GLASS	VINCENT
YAN	CANDLE	SOUP	FAITH	GRAVE

Joy Luck Club

TAITAI	RULES	TAIYUAN	NINGPO	DOUBLE
CHILD	GATES	SHANGHAI	MOLE	SHOSHANA
MAN	TED	FREE SPACE	FRANCISCO	CLAIR
SUN	ARCHITECT	CHOU	MEIMEI	SHOUT
HAROLD	RICE	WOOD	TAN	SHOU

Copyrighted

Joy Luck Club

SHANGHAI	PIANO	SUN	BOAT	YAN
CHOU	WOOD	WAVERLY	TYANYU	LENA
FOUR	TAN	FREE SPACE	SHOSHANA	GLASS
FOUND	JANICE	GATES	TAO	FAITH
LUCKY	SOUP	KWEILIN	BING	BIBLE

Joy Luck Club

RULES	CLAIR	RICH	LINDO	COLD
VOICE	HEAVEN	VINCENT	KINDS	CHUNG
DOUBLE	MOON	FREE SPACE	ART	TAITAI
ARNOLD	SHOU	SUYUAN	RED	HSU
MAGAZINES	CHESS	NINGPO	BLOOD	MEIMEI

Copyrighted

Joy Luck Club

BLOOD	LAUPO	CANDLE	HAROLD	ARCHITECT
TREES	COLD	RICE	BOAT	GRAVE
KWEILIN	TAITAI	FREE SPACE	HEAVEN	CHUNG
TAO	MOON	JOY	LEFTOVERS	CHINA
PIANO	WUTSING	FRANCISCO	OPIUM	SHOU

Joy Luck Club

WAVERLY	COOKIE	BRIGHTNESS	SHANGHAI	RULES
TICKETS	VOICE	GLASS	VINCENT	CHANG
JEWELRY	MEIMEI	FREE SPACE	CHESS	FAITH
WUSHI	BIBLE	HSU	YAN	NINGPO
QUALITY	LUCKY	TYANYU	LIFESAVERS	ART

Copyrighted

Joy Luck Club Vocabulary Word List

No.	Word	Clue/Definition
1.	ABANDONED	Deserted; left
2.	ACRID	Unpleasant to taste or smell
3.	BABBLING	Talking in nonsense
4.	BAZAARS	Street markets
5.	BELLOWS	Very loud, deep sounds
6.	BENEFACTOR	One who gives aid, esp. financial aid
7.	BENEVOLENT	Characterized by being or doing good
8.	BLOATED	Swelled up
9.	CANOPY	Roof-like covering
10.	CAUTIOUSLY	Carefully
11.	CHASM	Abyss; gorge; steep-sided hole
12.	CHASTISE	Criticize; punish; reprimand
13.	CICADAS	Insects that make high-pitched, droning sound
14.	COVENANT	Agreement
15.	CULTIVATE	Grow; encourage; promote
16.	CUNNING	Deceitful cleverness
17.	DECLARATION	Statement
18.	DEFTLY	Skillfully
19.	DESPICABLE	Deserving strong dislike; vile
20.	DEVIOUS	Sneaky
21.	DISTRACT	Divert
22.	DOWRY	Money or property brought by a bride to her new husband
23.	DRAB	Dull
24.	ELUDED	Escaped the understanding of
25.	ENCORE	Performance in response to the demand of the audience
26.	ENGULFED	Surrounded by something almost to the point of being lost in it
27.	ERUPTED	Became violently active; exploded
28.	EVICT	Put out, throw out, or expel
29.	EXASPERATED	At the end of patience; irritated
30.	EXTRACTED	Pulled out
31.	EXTRAVAGANT	Beyond necessary; luxurious
32.	FORAGE	Make a thorough search for
33.	FOYER	Entrance hall
34.	GENUINE	Real
35.	ILLUSION	False perception of reality
36.	INEVITABLE	Unavoidable; bound to happen
37.	INSOLENT	Arrogant; presumptuous and insulting
38.	INVADED	Entered by force to conquer
39.	INVENTORY	Taking a count of
40.	IRONIC	Contrary to what is expected
41.	IRRATIONAL	Not reasonable
42.	IRREVOCABLE	Can't be changed back
43.	LAMENTS	Regrets
44.	LOATHING	Great dislike
45.	LONGEVITY	Length of life
46.	MEAGER	Small or deficient in quantity
47.	MESMERIZING	Hypnotizing
48.	MUTE	Speechless
49.	OBSESSING	Thinking continually about something
50.	PARANOID	Having an extreme fear or distrust of others
51.	PARDON	Forgive

Copyrighted

No.	Word	Clue/Definition
52.	PENETRATE	Pierce; force into
53.	PODIATRIST	Foot doctor
54.	PORTER	Person who carries baggage
55.	POSTERITY	Future generations
56.	PREAMBLE	Introductory occurrence or statement
57.	PRECIOUS	Cherished; having value; beloved
58.	PRESUMPTUOUS	Excessively forward
59.	PRETENSE	False appearance
60.	PRISTINE	In perfect condition
61.	PRODIGY	Person with exceptional talents
62.	PROSPECT	Something expected
63.	RADICALLY	Departing from the norm; extremely
64.	REGAL	Royal
65.	REMNANTS	Left-overs
66.	REMORSE	Feeling of regret for one's misdeeds or sins
67.	REMORSEFUL	Regretful; sorrowful
68.	REVERE	Treat with respect
69.	REVIVING	Bringing back to life
70.	RUSE	A crafty plan
71.	SAUCINESS	Quality of being impossible to control or repress
72.	SCHEMING	Plotting to achieve an evil or illegal end
73.	SCURRIED	Scampered; hurried along
74.	SENTINEL	Guard
75.	SHABBY	Of substandard quality
76.	SIMMERING	Cooking just below the boiling point
77.	SIMPERING	Silly or self-conscious
78.	SMIRK	Offensively self-satisfied smile
79.	SOMBER	Serious
80.	SPOUSE	Husband or wife
81.	STAGNANT	Motionless
82.	STRATEGY	Plan
83.	STUNNED	Astounded; dazed
84.	SURVEYED	Looked over
85.	TAPERED	Gradually smaller from one end to the other
86.	TAUT	Tight
87.	THEOLOGY	Study of religion
88.	TOUTED	Publicly praised
89.	TRANSLUCENT	Allowing some light to pass through
90.	TRANSPARENT	Clear
91.	TRIVIAL	Of little importance
92.	UNANIMOUSLY	Completely in agreement
93.	UNCANNY	Mysteriously strange
94.	VAIN	Conceited; proud
95.	VEHEMENCE	Intensity
96.	VERBATIM	Word for word
97.	VIGOROUSLY	Done with force or energy
98.	VULNERABLE	Able to be hurt
99.	WANED	Decreased

Copyrighted

_____	1. Agreement
_____	2. In perfect condition
_____	3. Intensity
_____	4. Tight
_____	5. At the end of patience; irritated
_____	6. Street markets
_____	7. Guard
_____	8. Conceited; proud
_____	9. Motionless
_____	10. Great dislike
_____	11. False perception of reality
_____	12. Money or property brought by a bride to her new husband
_____	13. Departing from the norm; extremely
_____	14. Of little importance
_____	15. Deserted; left
_____	16. Contrary to what is expected
_____	17. Very loud, deep sounds
_____	18. Pierce; force into
_____	19. Dull
_____	20. Completely in agreement

Copyrighted

Joy Luck Club Vocabulary Fill In The Blanks 1 Answer Key

COVENANT	1. Agreement
PRISTINE	2. In perfect condition
VEHEMENCE	3. Intensity
TAUT	4. Tight
EXASPERATED	5. At the end of patience; irritated
BAZAARS	6. Street markets
SENTINEL	7. Guard
VAIN	8. Conceited; proud
STAGNANT	9. Motionless
LOATHING	10. Great dislike
ILLUSION	11. False perception of reality
DOWRY	12. Money or property brought by a bride to her new husband
RADICALLY	13. Departing from the norm; extremely
TRIVIAL	14. Of little importance
ABANDONED	15. Deserted; left
IRONIC	16. Contrary to what is expected
BELLOWS	17. Very loud, deep sounds
PENETRATE	18. Pierce; force into
DRAB	19. Dull
UNANIMOUSLY	20. Completely in agreement

Copyrighted

Joy Luck Club Vocabulary Fill In The Blanks 2

_____   1. Decreased

_____   2. Of substandard quality

_____   3. Completely in agreement

_____   4. Real

_____   5. Silly or self-conscious

_____   6. Beyond necessary; luxurious

_____   7. Money or property brought by a bride to her new husband

_____   8. Abyss; gorge; steep-sided hole

_____   9. Cherished; having value; beloved

_____   10. Word for word

_____   11. In perfect condition

_____   12. Regretful; sorrowful

_____   13. Small or deficient in quantity

_____   14. Bringing back to life

_____   15. Put out, throw out, or expel

_____   16. Pulled out

_____   17. Unpleasant to taste or smell

_____   18. Motionless

_____   19. Characterized by being or doing good

_____   20. Surrounded by something almost to the point of being lost in it

Copyrighted

WANED	1. Decreased
SHABBY	2. Of substandard quality
UNANIMOUSLY	3. Completely in agreement
GENUINE	4. Real
SIMPERING	5. Silly or self-conscious
EXTRAVAGANT	6. Beyond necessary; luxurious
DOWRY	7. Money or property brought by a bride to her new husband
CHASM	8. Abyss; gorge; steep-sided hole
PRECIOUS	9. Cherished; having value; beloved
VERBATIM	10. Word for word
PRISTINE	11. In perfect condition
REMORSEFUL	12. Regretful; sorrowful
MEAGER	13. Small or deficient in quantity
REVIVING	14. Bringing back to life
EVICT	15. Put out, throw out, or expel
EXTRACTED	16. Pulled out
ACRID	17. Unpleasant to taste or smell
STAGNANT	18. Motionless
BENEVOLENT	19. Characterized by being or doing good
ENGULFED	20. Surrounded by something almost to the point of being lost in it

Copyrighted

_____   1. Very loud, deep sounds

_____   2. Make a thorough search for

_____   3. Future generations

_____   4. Departing from the norm; extremely

_____   5. Swelled up

_____   6. Skillfully

_____   7. Regretful; sorrowful

_____   8. Serious

_____   9. Surrounded by something almost to the point of being lost in it

_____   10. Plotting to achieve an evil or illegal end

_____   11. Offensively self-satisfied smile

_____   12. Person who carries baggage

_____   13. Quality of being impossible to control or repress

_____   14. Guard

_____   15. Introductory occurrence or statement

_____   16. Intensity

_____   17. Deserving strong dislike; vile

_____   18. Excessively forward

_____   19. Sneaky

_____   20. Bringing back to life

Copyrighted

Joy Luck Club Vocabulary Fill In The Blanks 3 Answer Key

BELLOWS

1. Very loud, deep sounds

FORAGE

2. Make a thorough search for

POSTERITY

3. Future generations

RADICALLY

4. Departing from the norm; extremely

BLOATED

5. Swelled up

DEFTLY

6. Skillfully

REMORSEFUL

7. Regretful; sorrowful

SOMBER

8. Serious

ENGULFED

9. Surrounded by something almost to the point of being lost in it

SCHEMING

10. Plotting to achieve an evil or illegal end

SMIRK

11. Offensively self-satisfied smile

PORTER

12. Person who carries baggage

SAUCINESS

13. Quality of being impossible to control or repress

SENTINEL

14. Guard

PREAMBLE

15. Introductory occurrence or statement

VEHEMENCE

16. Intensity

DESPICABLE

17. Deserving strong dislike; vile

PRESUMPTUOUS

18. Excessively forward

DEVIOUS

19. Sneaky

REVIVING

20. Bringing back to life

Copyrighted

Joy Luck Club Vocabulary Fill In The Blanks 4

_____   1. Performance in response to the demand of the audience

_____   2. Word for word

_____   3. Person who carries baggage

_____   4. Beyond necessary; luxurious

_____   5. Tight

_____   6. Silly or self-conscious

_____   7. Study of religion

_____   8. Excessively forward

_____   9. Criticize; punish; reprimand

_____   10. Speechless

_____   11. Foot doctor

_____   12. Unavoidable; bound to happen

_____   13. Divert

_____   14. A crafty plan

_____   15. Future generations

_____   16. Completely in agreement

_____   17. Husband or wife

_____   18. Gradually smaller from one end to the other

_____   19. Unpleasant to taste or smell

_____   20. Allowing some light to pass through

Copyrighted

ENCORE	1. Performance in response to the demand of the audience
VERBATIM	2. Word for word
PORTER	3. Person who carries baggage
EXTRAVAGANT	4. Beyond necessary; luxurious
TAUT	5. Tight
SIMPERING	6. Silly or self-conscious
THEOLOGY	7. Study of religion
PRESUMPTUOUS	8. Excessively forward
CHASTISE	9. Criticize; punish; reprimand
MUTE	10. Speechless
PODIATRIST	11. Foot doctor
INEVITABLE	12. Unavoidable; bound to happen
DISTRACT	13. Divert
RUSE	14. A crafty plan
POSTERITY	15. Future generations
UNANIMOUSLY	16. Completely in agreement
SPOUSE	17. Husband or wife
TAPERED	18. Gradually smaller from one end to the other
ACRID	19. Unpleasant to taste or smell
TRANSLUCENT	20. Allowing some light to pass through

Copyrighted

Joy Luck Club Vocabulary Matching 1

____ 1. ABANDONED

____ 2. REMNANTS

____ 3. BENEFACTOR

____ 4. BLOATED

____ 5. SAUCINESS

____ 6. TAPERED

____ 7. PODIATRIST

____ 8. VERBATIM

____ 9. INEVITABLE

____10. SIMMERING

____11. REGAL

____12. SCURRIED

____13. VAIN

____14. UNANIMOUSLY

____15. WANED

____16. LONGEVITY

____17. ILLUSION

____18. TOUTED

____19. CULTIVATE

____20. PENETRATE

____21. BELLOWS

____22. IRONIC

____23. RUSE

____24. SENTINEL

____25. PRESUMPTUOUS

A. Quality of being impossible to control or repress

B. A crafty plan

C. Foot doctor

D. Gradually smaller from one end to the other

E. Grow; encourage; promote

F. Conceited; proud

G. Cooking just below the boiling point

H. One who gives aid, esp. financial aid

I. Very loud, deep sounds

J. Pierce; force into

K. Royal

L. Unavoidable; bound to happen

M. Guard

N. False perception of reality

O. Completely in agreement

P. Left-overs

Q. Excessively forward

R. Contrary to what is expected

S. Publicly praised

T. Length of life

U. Word for word

V. Decreased

W. Scampered; hurried along

X. Deserted; left

Y. Swelled up

Copyrighted

Joy Luck Club Vocabulary Matching 1 Answer Key

X - 1. ABANDONED

A. Quality of being impossible to control or repress

P - 2. REMNANTS

B. A crafty plan

H - 3. BENEFACTOR

C. Foot doctor

Y - 4. BLOATED

D. Gradually smaller from one end to the other

A - 5. SAUCINESS

E. Grow; encourage; promote

D - 6. TAPERED

F. Conceited; proud

C - 7. PODIATRIST

G. Cooking just below the boiling point

U - 8. VERBATIM

H. One who gives aid, esp. financial aid

L - 9. INEVITABLE

I. Very loud, deep sounds

G -10. SIMMERING

J. Pierce; force into

K -11. REGAL

K. Royal

W -12. SCURRIED

L. Unavoidable; bound to happen

F -13. VAIN

M. Guard

O -14. UNANIMOUSLY

N. False perception of reality

V -15. WANED

O. Completely in agreement

T -16. LONGEVITY

P. Left-overs

N -17. ILLUSION

Q. Excessively forward

S -18. TOUTED

R. Contrary to what is expected

E -19. CULTIVATE

S. Publicly praised

J - 20. PENETRATE

T. Length of life

I - 21. BELLOWS

U. Word for word

R -22. IRONIC

V. Decreased

B -23. RUSE

W. Scampered; hurried along

M -24. SENTINEL

X. Deserted; left

Q -25. PRESUMPTUOUS

Y. Swelled up

73
Copyrighted

Joy Luck Club Vocabulary Matching 2

___ 1. STUNNED   A. Allowing some light to pass through

___ 2. DEVIOUS   B. Contrary to what is expected

___ 3. CICADAS   C. Done with force or energy

___ 4. PREAMBLE   D. False perception of reality

___ 5. TRIVIAL   E. Of little importance

___ 6. UNANIMOUSLY   F. Roof-like covering

___ 7. CANOPY   G. Offensively self-satisfied smile

___ 8. LAMENTS   H. Astounded; dazed

___ 9. CUNNING   I. Dull

___10. BENEFACTOR   J. Sneaky

___11. SPOUSE   K. Beyond necessary; luxurious

___12. PROSPECT   L. Insects that make high-pitched, droning sound

___13. TRANSLUCENT   M. Taking a count of

___14. ACRID   N. Husband or wife

___15. PRODIGY   O. Became violently active; exploded

___16. ERUPTED   P. Put out, throw out, or expel

___17. EVICT   Q. Completely in agreement

___18. VIGOROUSLY   R. Introductory occurrence or statement

___19. PRISTINE   S. Unpleasant to taste or smell

___20. INVENTORY   T. Person with exceptional talents

___21. SMIRK   U. Deceitful cleverness

___22. DRAB   V. Something expected

___23. ILLUSION   W. One who gives aid, esp. financial aid

___24. EXTRAVAGANT   X. In perfect condition

___25. IRONIC   Y. Regrets

Copyrighted

Joy Luck Club Vocabulary Matching 2 Answer Key

H - 1. STUNNED   A. Allowing some light to pass through

J - 2. DEVIOUS   B. Contrary to what is expected

L - 3. CICADAS   C. Done with force or energy

R - 4. PREAMBLE   D. False perception of reality

E - 5. TRIVIAL   E. Of little importance

Q - 6. UNANIMOUSLY   F. Roof-like covering

F - 7. CANOPY   G. Offensively self-satisfied smile

Y - 8. LAMENTS   H. Astounded; dazed

U - 9. CUNNING   I. Dull

W - 10. BENEFACTOR   J. Sneaky

N - 11. SPOUSE   K. Beyond necessary; luxurious

V - 12. PROSPECT   L. Insects that make high-pitched, droning sound

A - 13. TRANSLUCENT   M. Taking a count of

S - 14. ACRID   N. Husband or wife

T - 15. PRODIGY   O. Became violently active; exploded

O - 16. ERUPTED   P. Put out, throw out, or expel

P - 17. EVICT   Q. Completely in agreement

C - 18. VIGOROUSLY   R. Introductory occurrence or statement

X - 19. PRISTINE   S. Unpleasant to taste or smell

M - 20. INVENTORY   T. Person with exceptional talents

G - 21. SMIRK   U. Deceitful cleverness

I - 22. DRAB   V. Something expected

D - 23. ILLUSION   W. One who gives aid, esp. financial aid

K - 24. EXTRAVAGANT   X. In perfect condition

B - 25. IRONIC   Y. Regrets

Copyrighted

Joy Luck Club Vocabulary Matching 3

___ 1. MESMERIZING   A. Left-overs

___ 2. SAUCINESS   B. Guard

___ 3. LAMENTS   C. Divert

___ 4. RUSE   D. Performance in response to the demand of the audience

___ 5. EXTRACTED   E. Deserving strong dislike; vile

___ 6. REMNANTS   F. Sneaky

___ 7. DEVIOUS   G. Characterized by being or doing good

___ 8. SENTINEL   H. A crafty plan

___ 9. BENEVOLENT   I. Done with force or energy

___10. ENCORE   J. Quality of being impossible to control or repress

___11. MUTE   K. Regrets

___12. CHASTISE   L. Person with exceptional talents

___13. PRODIGY   M. Agreement

___14. DECLARATION   N. Deceitful cleverness

___15. VIGOROUSLY   O. Criticize; punish; reprimand

___16. CUNNING   P. Statement

___17. BLOATED   Q. Talking in nonsense

___18. DISTRACT   R. Hypnotizing

___19. BABBLING   S. Speechless

___20. REMORSEFUL   T. Pulled out

___21. BELLOWS   U. Foot doctor

___22. COVENANT   V. Swelled up

___23. POSTERITY   W. Very loud, deep sounds

___24. DESPICABLE   X. Regretful; sorrowful

___25. PODIATRIST   Y. Future generations

Copyrighted

Joy Luck Club Vocabulary Matching 3 Answer Key

R - 1. MESMERIZING
J - 2. SAUCINESS
K - 3. LAMENTS
H - 4. RUSE
T - 5. EXTRACTED
A - 6. REMNANTS
F - 7. DEVIOUS
B - 8. SENTINEL
G - 9. BENEVOLENT
D -10. ENCORE
S -11. MUTE
O -12. CHASTISE
L -13. PRODIGY
P -14. DECLARATION
I - 15. VIGOROUSLY
N -16. CUNNING
V -17. BLOATED
C -18. DISTRACT
Q -19. BABBLING
X -20. REMORSEFUL
W -21. BELLOWS
M -22. COVENANT
Y -23. POSTERITY
E -24. DESPICABLE
U -25. PODIATRIST

A. Left-overs
B. Guard
C. Divert
D. Performance in response to the demand of the audience
E. Deserving strong dislike; vile
F. Sneaky
G. Characterized by being or doing good
H. A crafty plan
I. Done with force or energy
J. Quality of being impossible to control or repress
K. Regrets
L. Person with exceptional talents
M. Agreement
N. Deceitful cleverness
O. Criticize; punish; reprimand
P. Statement
Q. Talking in nonsense
R. Hypnotizing
S. Speechless
T. Pulled out
U. Foot doctor
V. Swelled up
W. Very loud, deep sounds
X. Regretful; sorrowful
Y. Future generations

Copyrighted

Joy Luck Club Vocabulary Matching 4

___ 1. DEFTLY   A. Scampered; hurried along

___ 2. INVENTORY   B. Taking a count of

___ 3. VEHEMENCE   C. False perception of reality

___ 4. REMORSEFUL   D. Person who carries baggage

___ 5. SIMPERING   E. Plan

___ 6. ENGULFED   F. Of substandard quality

___ 7. PORTER   G. Abyss; gorge; steep-sided hole

___ 8. ELUDED   H. Escaped the understanding of

___ 9. ILLUSION   I. Serious

___10. STRATEGY   J. Silly or self-conscious

___11. INEVITABLE   K. Regretful; sorrowful

___12. CUNNING   L. Having an extreme fear or distrust of others

___13. PARANOID   M. Skillfully

___14. SHABBY   N. Introductory occurrence or statement

___15. WANED   O. Hypnotizing

___16. OBSESSING   P. Deceitful cleverness

___17. PRECIOUS   Q. Unavoidable; bound to happen

___18. EXASPERATED   R. Intensity

___19. CHASM   S. Offensively self-satisfied smile

___20. PREAMBLE   T. Cherished; having value; beloved

___21. SOMBER   U. Decreased

___22. MESMERIZING   V. Surrounded by something almost to the point of being
                                 lost in it

___23. SMIRK   W. Thinking continually about something

___24. SCURRIED   X. At the end of patience; irritated

___25. CHASTISE   Y. Criticize; punish; reprimand

Copyrighted

Joy Luck Club Vocabulary Matching 4 Answer Key

M - 1. DEFTLY

B - 2. INVENTORY

R - 3. VEHEMENCE

K - 4. REMORSEFUL

J - 5. SIMPERING

V - 6. ENGULFED

D - 7. PORTER

H - 8. ELUDED

C - 9. ILLUSION

E -10. STRATEGY

Q -11. INEVITABLE

P -12. CUNNING

L -13. PARANOID

F -14. SHABBY

U -15. WANED

W -16. OBSESSING

T -17. PRECIOUS

X -18. EXASPERATED

G -19. CHASM

N -20. PREAMBLE

I - 21. SOMBER

O -22. MESMERIZING

S -23. SMIRK

A -24. SCURRIED

Y -25. CHASTISE

A. Scampered; hurried along

B. Taking a count of

C. False perception of reality

D. Person who carries baggage

E. Plan

F. Of substandard quality

G. Abyss; gorge; steep-sided hole

H. Escaped the understanding of

I. Serious

J. Silly or self-conscious

K. Regretful; sorrowful

L. Having an extreme fear or distrust of others

M. Skillfully

N. Introductory occurrence or statement

O. Hypnotizing

P. Deceitful cleverness

Q. Unavoidable; bound to happen

R. Intensity

S. Offensively self-satisfied smile

T. Cherished; having value; beloved

U. Decreased

V. Surrounded by something almost to the point of being lost in it

W. Thinking continually about something

X. At the end of patience; irritated

Y. Criticize; punish; reprimand

Copyrighted

Joy Luck Club Vocabulary Magic Squares 1

Match the definition with the vocabulary word. Put your answers in the magic squares below. When your answers are correct, all columns and rows will add to the same number.

A. POSTERITY
B. OBSESSING
C. EXTRACTED
D. PRECIOUS
E. DEFTLY
F. SIMMERING

G. WANED
H. VEHEMENCE
I. SHABBY
J. REGAL
K. INSOLENT
L. RUSE

M. TOUTED
N. PORTER
O. CHASM
P. BENEFACTOR

1. Thinking continually about something

2. Decreased

3. Arrogant; presumptuous and insulting

4. Person who carries baggage

5. Publicly praised

6. A crafty plan

7. Intensity

8. Future generations

9. One who gives aid, esp. financial aid

10. Of substandard quality

11. Skillfully

12. Cherished; having value; beloved

13. Pulled out

14. Cooking just below the boiling point

15. Royal

16. Abyss; gorge; steep-sided hole

A=	B=	C=	D=
E=	F=	G=	H=
I=	J=	K=	L=
M=	N=	O=	P=

Copyrighted

Joy Luck Club Vocabulary Magic Squares 1 Answer Key

Match the definition with the vocabulary word. Put your answers in the magic squares below. When your answers are correct, all columns and rows will add to the same number.

A. POSTERITY
B. OBSESSING
C. EXTRACTED
D. PRECIOUS
E. DEFTLY
F. SIMMERING

G. WANED
H. VEHEMENCE
I. SHABBY
J. REGAL
K. INSOLENT
L. RUSE

M. TOUTED
N. PORTER
O. CHASM
P. BENEFACTOR

1. Thinking continually about something

2. Decreased

3. Arrogant; presumptuous and insulting

4. Person who carries baggage

5. Publicly praised

6. A crafty plan

7. Intensity

8. Future generations

9. One who gives aid, esp. financial aid

10. Of substandard quality

11. Skillfully

12. Cherished; having value; beloved

13. Pulled out

14. Cooking just below the boiling point

15. Royal

16. Abyss; gorge; steep-sided hole

A=8	B=1	C=13	D=12
E=11	F=14	G=2	H=7
I=10	J=15	K=3	L=6
M=5	N=4	O=16	P=9

Copyrighted

Joy Luck Club Vocabulary Magic Squares 2

Match the definition with the vocabulary word. Put your answers in the magic squares below. When your answers are correct, all columns and rows will add to the same number.

A. RADICALLY
B. SCHEMING
C. PROSPECT
D. BENEFACTOR
E. VAIN
F. CAUTIOUSLY

G. CHASM
H. TRANSPARENT
I. ENCORE
J. EXTRAVAGANT
K. VERBATIM
L. MEAGER

M. TAPERED
N. TAUT
O. MUTE
P. WANED

1. Gradually smaller from one end to the other
2. Carefully
3. Clear
4. Speechless
5. Small or deficient in quantity
6. Something expected
7. Departing from the norm; extremely
8. Beyond necessary; luxurious

9. Word for word
10. One who gives aid, esp. financial aid
11. Plotting to achieve an evil or illegal end
12. Performance in response to the demand of the audience
13. Tight
14. Conceited; proud
15. Abyss; gorge; steep-sided hole
16. Decreased

A=	B=	C=	D=
E=	F=	G=	H=
I=	J=	K=	L=
M=	N=	O=	P=

Copyrighted

Joy Luck Club Vocabulary Magic Squares 2 Answer Key

Match the definition with the vocabulary word. Put your answers in the magic squares below. When your answers are correct, all columns and rows will add to the same number.

A. RADICALLY
B. SCHEMING
C. PROSPECT
D. BENEFACTOR
E. VAIN
F. CAUTIOUSLY

G. CHASM
H. TRANSPARENT
I. ENCORE
J. EXTRAVAGANT
K. VERBATIM
L. MEAGER

M. TAPERED
N. TAUT
O. MUTE
P. WANED

1. Gradually smaller from one end to the other
2. Carefully
3. Clear
4. Speechless
5. Small or deficient in quantity
6. Something expected
7. Departing from the norm; extremely
8. Beyond necessary; luxurious
9. Word for word
10. One who gives aid, esp. financial aid
11. Plotting to achieve an evil or illegal end
12. Performance in response to the demand of the audience
13. Tight
14. Conceited; proud
15. Abyss; gorge; steep-sided hole
16. Decreased

A=7	B=11	C=6	D=10
E=14	F=2	G=15	H=3
I=12	J=8	K=9	L=5
M=1	N=13	O=4	P=16

Copyrighted

Joy Luck Club Vocabulary Magic Squares 3

Match the definition with the vocabulary word. Put your answers in the magic squares below. When your answers are correct, all columns and rows will add to the same number.

A. INSOLENT
B. THEOLOGY
C. REVIVING
D. CUNNING
E. POSTERITY
F. CANOPY

G. RUSE
H. STRATEGY
I. TRANSPARENT
J. PRISTINE
K. PENETRATE
L. STAGNANT

M. INVENTORY
N. SIMMERING
O. BLOATED
P. ACRID

1. Bringing back to life

2. In perfect condition

3. Roof-like covering

4. Swelled up

5. Unpleasant to taste or smell

6. Future generations

7. Clear

8. Deceitful cleverness

9. Taking a count of

10. Plan

11. Motionless

12. Arrogant; presumptuous and insulting

13. Study of religion

14. Pierce; force into

15. A crafty plan

16. Cooking just below the boiling point

A=	B=	C=	D=
E=	F=	G=	H=
I=	J=	K=	L=
M=	N=	O=	P=

Copyrighted

Joy Luck Club Vocabulary Magic Squares 3 Answer Key

Match the definition with the vocabulary word. Put your answers in the magic squares below. When your answers are correct, all columns and rows will add to the same number.

A. INSOLENT
B. THEOLOGY
C. REVIVING
D. CUNNING
E. POSTERITY
F. CANOPY

G. RUSE
H. STRATEGY
I. TRANSPARENT
J. PRISTINE
K. PENETRATE
L. STAGNANT

M. INVENTORY
N. SIMMERING
O. BLOATED
P. ACRID

1. Bringing back to life

2. In perfect condition

3. Roof-like covering

4. Swelled up

5. Unpleasant to taste or smell

6. Future generations

7. Clear

8. Deceitful cleverness

9. Taking a count of

10. Plan

11. Motionless

12. Arrogant; presumptuous and insulting

13. Study of religion

14. Pierce; force into

15. A crafty plan

16. Cooking just below the boiling point

A=12	B=13	C=1	D=8
E=6	F=3	G=15	H=10
I=7	J=2	K=14	L=11
M=9	N=16	O=4	P=5

Copyrighted

Joy Luck Club Vocabulary Magic Squares 4

Match the definition with the vocabulary word. Put your answers in the magic squares below. When your answers are correct, all columns and rows will add to the same number.

A. TOUTED
B. ILLUSION
C. STAGNANT
D. TRIVIAL
E. VEHEMENCE
F. ACRID

G. EVICT
H. CHASM
I. BABBLING
J. DECLARATION
K. SIMPERING
L. BENEVOLENT

M. INVADED
N. DRAB
O. ENCORE
P. STRATEGY

1. Unpleasant to taste or smell
2. Talking in nonsense
3. Performance in response to the demand of the audience
4. Of little importance
5. Entered by force to conquer
6. False perception of reality
7. Abyss; gorge; steep-sided hole
8. Silly or self-conscious

9. Motionless
10. Plan
11. Statement
12. Intensity
13. Characterized by being or doing good
14. Put out, throw out, or expel
15. Publicly praised
16. Dull

A=	B=	C=	D=
E=	F=	G=	H=
I=	J=	K=	L=
M=	N=	O=	P=

Copyrighted

Joy Luck Club Vocabulary Magic Squares 4 Answer Key

Match the definition with the vocabulary word. Put your answers in the magic squares below. When your answers are correct, all columns and rows will add to the same number.

A. TOUTED
B. ILLUSION
C. STAGNANT
D. TRIVIAL
E. VEHEMENCE
F. ACRID

G. EVICT
H. CHASM
I. BABBLING
J. DECLARATION
K. SIMPERING
L. BENEVOLENT

M. INVADED
N. DRAB
O. ENCORE
P. STRATEGY

1. Unpleasant to taste or smell
2. Talking in nonsense
3. Performance in response to the demand of the audience
4. Of little importance
5. Entered by force to conquer
6. False perception of reality
7. Abyss; gorge; steep-sided hole
8. Silly or self-conscious

9. Motionless
10. Plan
11. Statement
12. Intensity
13. Characterized by being or doing good
14. Put out, throw out, or expel
15. Publicly praised
16. Dull

A=15	B=6	C=9	D=4
E=12	F=1	G=14	H=7
I=2	J=11	K=8	L=13
M=5	N=16	O=3	P=10

Copyrighted

Joy Luck Club Vocabulary Word Search 1

Words are placed backwards, forward, diagonally, up and down. Clues listed below can help you find the words. Circle the hidden vocabulary words in the maze.

```
E  T  A  V  I  T  L  U  C  P  R  O  D  I  G  Y  D  G  D  Y
D  R  C  N  V  F  L  C  N  F  R  E  L  U  D  E  D  D  E  T
H  I  U  J  I  R  O  N  I  C  F  E  F  F  T  Z  B  I  V  J
T  V  N  P  P  E  D  Y  V  W  O  W  T  U  H  Y  D  R  I  H
K  I  N  Z  T  V  R  R  E  L  R  J  O  E  G  E  V  C  O  R
S  A  I  Z  D  E  C  L  A  R  A  T  I  O  N  S  T  A  U  T
U  L  N  Z  B  R  D  G  E  E  G  D  L  N  I  S  Q  S  S  Y
O  S  G  M  B  E  E  T  T  G  E  L  U  F  V  L  E  F  G  Q
I  M  O  N  K  R  R  R  U  A  P  T  A  S  I  R  T  E  T  T
C  S  E  N  C  O  R  E  M  E  S  S  C  M  V  W  T  D  N  H
E  H  P  O  P  S  T  M  X  M  P  U  T  C  E  A  A  E  A  G
R  D  A  I  C  M  K  O  Q  O  R  L  A  R  N  L  N  N  N  K
P  R  R  S  Q  I  P  R  U  R  Y  V  D  T  G  O  T  I  E  D
G  A  D  U  M  R  H  S  I  P  Q  E  S  E  S  N  L  S  V  D
L  B  O  L  Z  K  E  E  O  B  F  Y  Q  N  F  B  A  K  O  T
X  S  N  L  P  C  D  N  M  P  C  E  I  Q  B  T  J  N  C  V
S  E  V  I  C  T  A  P  E  R  E  D  V  A  I  N  L  Y  T  G
N  Y  P  C  S  C  H  E  M  I  N  G  B  D  O  W  R  Y  N  H
M  G  R  L  M  F  W  W  J  Y  N  G  V  V  R  M  W  C  J  D
```

A crafty plan (4)
Abyss; gorge; steep-sided hole (5)
Agreement (8)
Arrogant; presumptuous and insulting (8)
Astounded; dazed (7)
Became violently active; exploded (7)
Bringing back to life (8)
Cherished; having value; beloved (8)
Conceited; proud (4)
Contrary to what is expected (6)
Deceitful cleverness (7)
Decreased (5)
Dull (4)
Entrance hall (5)
Escaped the understanding of (6)
False appearance (8)
False perception of reality (8)
Feeling of regret for one's misdeeds or sins (7)
Forgive (6)
Gradually smaller from one end to the other (7)
Grow; encourage; promote (9)
Husband or wife (6)
Looked over (8)
Make a thorough search for (6)
Money or property brought by a bride to her new husband (5)

Motionless (8)
Of little importance (7)
Offensively self-satisfied smile (5)
Performance in response to the demand of the audience (6)
Person who carries baggage (6)
Person with exceptional talents (7)
Plan (8)
Plotting to achieve an evil or illegal end (8)
Publicly praised (6)
Put out, throw out, or expel (5)
Regrets (7)
Roof-like covering (6)
Royal (5)
Scampered; hurried along (8)
Serious (6)
Skillfully (6)
Small or deficient in quantity (6)
Sneaky (7)
Speechless (4)
Statement (11)
Talking in nonsense (8)
Tight (4)
Treat with respect (6)
Unpleasant to taste or smell (5)

Copyrighted

Joy Luck Club Vocabulary Word Search 1 Answer Key

Words are placed backwards, forward, diagonally, up and down. Clues listed below can help you find the words. Circle the hidden vocabulary words in the maze.

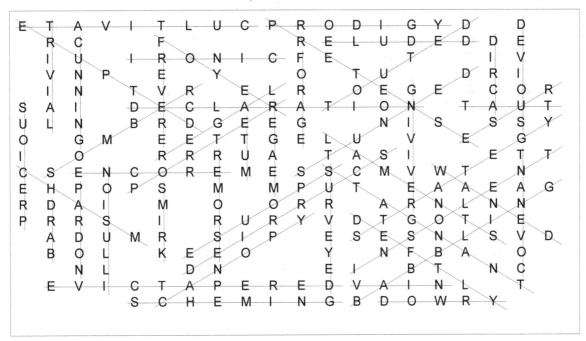

A crafty plan (4)
Abyss; gorge; steep-sided hole (5)
Agreement (8)
Arrogant; presumptuous and insulting (8)
Astounded; dazed (7)
Became violently active; exploded (7)
Bringing back to life (8)
Cherished; having value; beloved (8)
Conceited; proud (4)
Contrary to what is expected (6)
Deceitful cleverness (7)
Decreased (5)
Dull (4)
Entrance hall (5)
Escaped the understanding of (6)
False appearance (8)
False perception of reality (8)
Feeling of regret for one's misdeeds or sins (7)
Forgive (6)
Gradually smaller from one end to the other (7)
Grow; encourage; promote (9)
Husband or wife (6)
Looked over (8)
Make a thorough search for (6)
Money or property brought by a bride to her new husband (5)

Motionless (8)
Of little importance (7)
Offensively self-satisfied smile (5)
Performance in response to the demand of the audience (6)
Person who carries baggage (6)
Person with exceptional talents (7)
Plan (8)
Plotting to achieve an evil or illegal end (8)
Publicly praised (6)
Put out, throw out, or expel (5)
Regrets (7)
Roof-like covering (6)
Royal (5)
Scampered; hurried along (8)
Serious (6)
Skillfully (6)
Small or deficient in quantity (6)
Sneaky (7)
Speechless (4)
Statement (11)
Talking in nonsense (8)
Tight (4)
Treat with respect (6)
Unpleasant to taste or smell (5)

Copyrighted

Joy Luck Club Vocabulary Word Search 2

Words are placed backwards, forward, diagonally, up and down. Clues listed below can help you find the words. Circle the hidden vocabulary words in the maze.

```
P  E  N  E  T  R  A  T  E  D  E  T  A  R  E  P  S  A  X  E
O  P  O  C  G  A  X  C  K  N  N  G  N  Q  P  V  B  F  E  Y
S  A  D  N  Q  S  P  R  F  J  C  H  A  S  M  A  I  G  N  C
T  R  R  E  X  I  I  E  S  O  O  D  J  V  N  B  M  C  I  L
E  A  A  M  C  M  B  Q  R  B  R  C  R  D  G  E  U  Q  T  B
R  N  P  E  S  M  A  D  A  E  E  A  O  A  I  L  T  Z  S  D
I  O  X  H  S  E  B  E  A  B  D  N  G  N  B  L  E  R  I  W
T  I  N  E  A  R  B  B  S  Z  H  E  K  E  E  C  O  S  E  R  Q
Y  D  Q  V  U  I  L  P  A  D  N  V  G  F  I  W  L  M  P  Z
C  R  V  K  C  N  I  I  B  V  I  D  G  Y  C  S  G  O  O  J
S  C  U  C  I  G  N  C  N  T  R  I  V  I  A  L  D  R  R  H
S  K  T  S  N  D  G  A  A  D  S  W  G  T  D  I  Y  S  T  D
J  T  P  R  E  A  M  B  L  E  Y  P  O  N  A  C  G  E  E  H
R  N  U  T  S  H  L  L  A  N  S  X  O  T  S  U  E  F  R  K
D  E  U  N  S  E  J  E  G  A  M  O  R  U  Q  D  T  O  A  H
C  O  V  E  N  A  N  T  E  W  B  I  M  N  S  L  A  Y  C  B
T  G  W  E  Y  E  Z  L  R  J  S  M  I  B  Y  E  R  E  R  Y
G  X  Q  R  R  M  D  I  S  T  R  A  C  T  E  L  T  R  I  M
V  P  D  E  Y  E  V  R  U  S  V  B  K  J  D  R  S  S  D  M
```

A crafty plan (4)
Abyss; gorge; steep-sided hole (5)
Agreement (8)
Astounded; dazed (7)
At the end of patience; irritated (11)
Conceited; proud (4)
Cooking just below the boiling point (9)
Decreased (5)
Deserted; left (9)
Deserving strong dislike; vile (10)
Divert (8)
Dull (4)
Entrance hall (5)
Feeling of regret for one's misdeeds or sins (7)
Foot doctor (10)
Forgive (6)
Future generations (9)
Gradually smaller from one end to the other (7)
Having an extreme fear or distrust of others (8)
Husband or wife (6)
In perfect condition (8)
Insects that make high-pitched, droning sound (7)
Intensity (9)
Introductory occurrence or statement (8)
Looked over (8)

Make a thorough search for (6)
Money or property brought by a bride to her new husband (5)
Of little importance (7)
Offensively self-satisfied smile (5)
Performance in response to the demand of the audience (6)
Person who carries baggage (6)
Pierce; force into (9)
Plan (8)
Publicly praised (6)
Put out, throw out, or expel (5)
Quality of being impossible to control or repress (9)
Roof-like covering (6)
Royal (5)
Serious (6)
Skillfully (6)
Speechless (4)
Street markets (7)
Talking in nonsense (8)
Tight (4)
Treat with respect (6)
Unavoidable; bound to happen (10)
Unpleasant to taste or smell (5)
Very loud, deep sounds (7)

Copyrighted

Joy Luck Club Vocabulary Word Search 2 Answer Key

Words are placed backwards, forward, diagonally, up and down. Clues listed below can help you find the words. Circle the hidden vocabulary words in the maze.

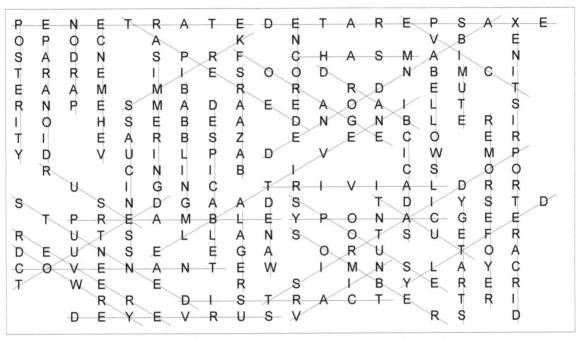

A crafty plan (4)
Abyss; gorge; steep-sided hole (5)
Agreement (8)
Astounded; dazed (7)
At the end of patience; irritated (11)
Conceited; proud (4)
Cooking just below the boiling point (9)
Decreased (5)
Deserted; left (9)
Deserving strong dislike; vile (10)
Divert (8)
Dull (4)
Entrance hall (5)
Feeling of regret for one's misdeeds or sins (7)
Foot doctor (10)
Forgive (6)
Future generations (9)
Gradually smaller from one end to the other (7)
Having an extreme fear or distrust of others (8)
Husband or wife (6)
In perfect condition (8)
Insects that make high-pitched, droning sound (7)
Intensity (9)
Introductory occurrence or statement (8)
Looked over (8)

Make a thorough search for (6)
Money or property brought by a bride to her new husband (5)
Of little importance (7)
Offensively self-satisfied smile (5)
Performance in response to the demand of the audience (6)
Person who carries baggage (6)
Pierce; force into (9)
Plan (8)
Publicly praised (6)
Put out, throw out, or expel (5)
Quality of being impossible to control or repress (9)
Roof-like covering (6)
Royal (5)
Serious (6)
Skillfully (6)
Speechless (4)
Street markets (7)
Talking in nonsense (8)
Tight (4)
Treat with respect (6)
Unavoidable; bound to happen (10)
Unpleasant to taste or smell (5)
Very loud, deep sounds (7)

Copyrighted

```
T R I V I A L N Y P O N A C R M P J Y W
S W O L L E B K Y R L A G E R N A R G C
L S L M Q L E S X E F L Y R V N R N U F
E X L A O U S J A S X O N E E L A N Y J
T X S A M D U Z S U F N S V Y M N G G Q
N Q T A P E R E D M C P R E C I O U S N
G E A R F D N T U P I I S R N L I R L N
D T G X A M C T C T P R N G O T D P S C
S A N F V C E D S U R R K E D P I W X E
S V A T O U T E D O E C H A S M Z N Y J
C I N C M J S E X U A T Q V I S N T E Y
H T T S R H B I D S M M S N M Z I S S L
E L C S O I S V M F B Q S C P V V G I F
M U S Y H M D B D M L L Y G E T A R T S
I C N U D A B L O E E S E G R N E T S S
N R T C R P B E W A B R N C I E V A A D
G W N I A V Z B R G T O I R N L I U H V
P C A R B N E S Y E L N U N G O C T C V
Y T D N T M N Y E R O C N E G S T Q M G
P O R T E R R Y E R Q R E D E N N U T S
N I N V A D E D I D Q Z G Y G I D O R P
```

ACRID

BELLOWS

BLOATED

CANOPY

CHASM

CHASTISE

CULTIVATE

CUNNING

DOWRY

DRAB

ELUDED

ENCORE

EVICT

EXTRACTED

FOYER

GENUINE

INSOLENT

INVADED

IRONIC

LAMENTS

LONGEVITY

MEAGER

MUTE

PARANOID

PARDON

PORTER

PREAMBLE

PRECIOUS

PRESUMPTUOUS

PRODIGY

REGAL

REMORSE

REVERE

RUSE

SAUCINESS

SCHEMING

SENTINEL

SHABBY

SIMMERING

SIMPERING

SMIRK

SOMBER

STAGNANT

STRATEGY

STUNNED

SURVEYED

TAPERED

TAUT

THEOLOGY

TOUTED

TRIVIAL

UNCANNY

VAIN

WANED

92
Copyrighted

Joy Luck Club Vocabulary Word Search 3 Answer Key

```
T R I V I A L   Y P O N A C R   P
S W O L L E B   R L A G E R   A       C
    L     L E S   R     Y R E   R       U
E   A O U S   A S   F   S V   M A N   Y
    X S A M D U   S U F C P R E C I O U S
    T A P E R E D M   C P R   R N L I R
    E R   D N   U   I P   R N G O T D   S
D   T G   A   T   T   P R N K E   I     E
  S A N   C E   S   U R E C H A S M   N Y
S C I T O U T E D O   E U A T   I S   T E
C H N C   S R   S E   U A   M   P   I   S L
H E T S R   I   I D S M B   M V   I S
E M U S H M D   D M L E   Y G E T A R T S
M I C N U D B   O E E   E G R N E T S
I N C R P B E W   R N C I N E V A H
N G W N I A V   B R Y E L N U N G O C T C
  A R B N E   N Y E R O C N E G S T
  D N   N Y E R     E D E N N U T S
P O R T E R R Y E R   G Y G I D O R P
N I N V A D E D I D
```

ACRID

BELLOWS

BLOATED

CANOPY

CHASM

CHASTISE

CULTIVATE

CUNNING

DOWRY

DRAB

ELUDED

ENCORE

EVICT

EXTRACTED

FOYER

GENUINE

INSOLENT

INVADED

IRONIC

LAMENTS

LONGEVITY

MEAGER

MUTE

PARANOID

PARDON

PORTER

PREAMBLE

PRECIOUS

PRESUMPTUOUS

PRODIGY

REGAL

REMORSE

REVERE

RUSE

SAUCINESS

SCHEMING

SENTINEL

SHABBY

SIMMERING

SIMPERING

SMIRK

SOMBER

STAGNANT

STRATEGY

STUNNED

SURVEYED

TAPERED

TAUT

THEOLOGY

TOUTED

TRIVIAL

UNCANNY

VAIN

WANED

Copyrighted

```
M  U  T  E  R  E  V  E  R  E  E  B  C  S  U  O  I  V  E  D
R  X  R  R  E  S  B  D  E  X  G  Z  H  V  O  Y  Y  F  R  V
E  Z  S  O  G  L  W  W  N  T  A  V  T  R  P  M  Z  P  D  L
M  U  N  C  A  N  N  Y  I  R  R  E  V  O  C  A  B  L  E  B
N  E  P  N  E  T  G  Z  U  A  O  T  N  S  U  A  E  E  I  L
A  T  S  E  M  O  S  S  N  V  F  A  E  A  R  T  N  G  R  F
N  R  S  M  L  A  E  Z  E  A  C  R  V  D  I  B  E  S  R  B
T  R  E  O  E  C  H  X  G  G  D  T  I  A  N  L  V  D  U  K
S  E  E  L  D  R  A  W  J  A  O  E  C  C  V  O  O  I  C  B
P  H  R  V  U  I  I  U  F  N  W  N  T  I  A  A  L  L  S  R
T  O  P  U  I  D  C  Z  T  T  R  E  E  C  D  T  E  L  P  N
T  F  S  R  P  V  E  H  I  I  Y  P  S  W  E  E  N  U  O  N
A  N  O  T  O  T  I  D  A  N  O  G  I  T  D  D  T  S  R  D
R  B  V  Y  E  D  E  N  F  S  G  U  T  R  A  Y  Z  I  T  Y
E  L  A  G  E  R  I  D  G  T  M  J  S  T  O  G  G  O  E  X
M  M  I  N  E  R  I  G  P  U  F  T  A  L  G  N  N  N  R  T
O  R  N  P  D  Q  N  T  Y  N  N  U  H  W  Y  I  I  A  C  V
R  P  A  R  D  O  N  B  Y  N  T  F  C  C  A  N  D  C  N  X
S  T  L  A  M  E  N  T  S  E  H  C  O  V  E  N  A  N  T  C
E  S  U  O  P  S  R  E  K  D  S  M  I  R  K  U  E  K  M  C
E  N  G  U  L  F  E  D  D  E  F  T  L  Y  W  C  D  D  N  J
```

ABANDONED	DRAB	LAMENTS	RUSE
ACRID	ELUDED	MEAGER	SCURRIED
BENEVOLENT	ENCORE	MESMERIZING	SMIRK
BLOATED	ENGULFED	MUTE	SOMBER
CANOPY	ERUPTED	PARDON	SPOUSE
CAUTIOUSLY	EVICT	PENETRATE	STAGNANT
CHASM	EXTRAVAGANT	PORTER	STUNNED
CHASTISE	FORAGE	POSTERITY	TAPERED
CICADAS	FOYER	PRODIGY	TAUT
COVENANT	GENUINE	REGAL	THEOLOGY
CUNNING	ILLUSION	REMNANTS	TOUTED
DEFTLY	INVADED	REMORSE	UNCANNY
DEVIOUS	IRONIC	REVERE	VAIN
DOWRY	IRREVOCABLE	REVIVING	WANED

Copyrighted

```
M U T E R E V E R E E E           S U O I V E D
R       R   E           E   X G       O   Y
        R   E           E   X G   T   P   M           D
M U N C A N N Y   I R R E V O C A B L E
  N     E   N   G       U   A   O   T   N   S   U   A   E   E   I
      S   E   M   O   S   N   V   F   A   R   D   I   B   E   R
        M   L   A   E       N   E   G   D   T   I   A   N   B   L   V   D
  R   E   O   E   C       G   G   D   T   A   C   C   I   V   O   O   I
  S   E   E   L   R   A       A   O   E   N   V   A   D   L   L   I
P   H   R   V   U   I   U       T   W   N   E   T   A   L   D   N   R
T   O   P   U   I   D   C   Z   T       R   Y   P   S   I   E   D   I   U
    F   S   R   P   V   E   H   I   I       N   O       T   D   D   L   S   P
A       O   T   O   T   I   D   A   N       S   G   I   T   R   A       O
R   B   V   Y   E   D   E   N       S   U   G   U   T   S   R   A       I
E   L   A   G   E   R   I   D   G   T   M       S   T   O   G       N   R
M   I   N   E   R   I   G       Y       U   A   L   N   N
O   N   P   D       T   Y   N       U   H   W   Y   I   I
R   P   A   R   D   O   N       Y   N   T   C   A   N   C   N
S   T   L   A   M   E   N   T   S   E       C   O   V   E   N   A   N   T   T
E   S   U   O   P   S       E   D   S   M   I   R   K   U   E
E   N   G   U   L   F   E   D   D   E   F   T   L   Y       C       D
```

ABANDONED	DRAB	LAMENTS	RUSE
ACRID	ELUDED	MEAGER	SCURRIED
BENEVOLENT	ENCORE	MESMERIZING	SMIRK
BLOATED	ENGULFED	MUTE	SOMBER
CANOPY	ERUPTED	PARDON	SPOUSE
CAUTIOUSLY	EVICT	PENETRATE	STAGNANT
CHASM	EXTRAVAGANT	PORTER	STUNNED
CHASTISE	FORAGE	POSTERITY	TAPERED
CICADAS	FOYER	PRODIGY	TAUT
COVENANT	GENUINE	REGAL	THEOLOGY
CUNNING	ILLUSION	REMNANTS	TOUTED
DEFTLY	INVADED	REMORSE	UNCANNY
DEVIOUS	IRONIC	REVERE	VAIN
DOWRY	IRREVOCABLE	REVIVING	WANED

Copyrighted

Joy Luck Club Vocabulary Crossword 1

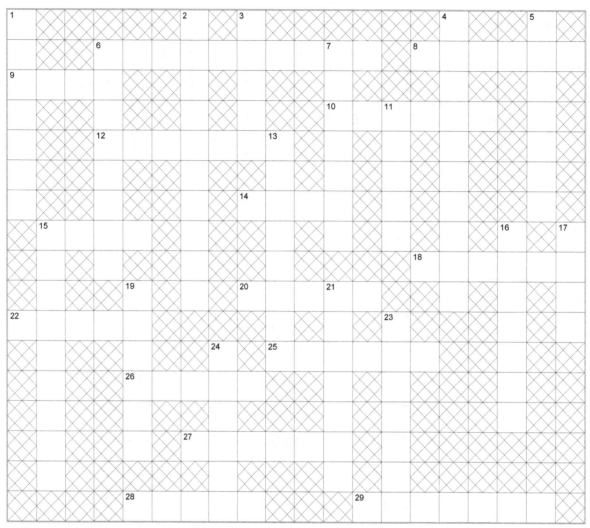

Across
6. Done with force or energy
8. Skillfully
9. Speechless
10. Small or deficient in quantity
12. Street markets
14. Tight
15. Conceited; proud
18. Person who carries baggage
20. Decreased
22. Royal
25. Publicly praised
26. Money or property brought by a bride to her new husband
27. Performance in response to the demand of the audience
28. Put out, throw out, or expel
29. Sneaky

Down
1. Feeling of regret for one's misdeeds or sins
2. Foot doctor
3. Entrance hall
4. One who gives aid, esp. financial aid
5. Swelled up
6. Word for word
7. Regrets
11. Unpleasant to taste or smell
13. Motionless
15. Intensity
16. Astounded; dazed
17. Dull
19. Escaped the understanding of
21. Became violently active; exploded
23. Real
24. Contrary to what is expected

.

Copyrighted

1 R				2 P		3 F				4 B			5 B	
E	6 V	I	G	O	R	O	U	S	7 L	Y	8 D	E	F	T	L	Y
9 M	U	T	E		D		Y		A		N		O	
O		R		I		E		10 M	E	11 A	G	E	R		A
R		12 B	A	Z	A	A	R	13 S		E		C		F		T
S		A		T			T		N		R		A		E
E		T		R		14 T	A	U	T		I		C		D
15 V	A	I	N		I		G		S		D		T	16 S	17 D
E	M		S		N					18 P	O	R	T	E	R
H		19 E	T		20 W	A	N	E	D		R		U		A
22 R	E	G	A	L		N		R		23 G		N		B
M		U		24 I		25 T	O	U	T	E	D		N
E		26 D	O	W	R	Y		P		N		E
N		E		O			T		U		D
C		D		27 E	N	C	O	R	E		I
E				I		D		N
28 E	V	I	C	T		29 D	E	V	I	O	U	S

Across

6. Done with force or energy
8. Skillfully
9. Speechless
10. Small or deficient in quantity
12. Street markets
14. Tight
15. Conceited; proud
18. Person who carries baggage
20. Decreased
22. Royal
25. Publicly praised
26. Money or property brought by a bride to her new husband
27. Performance in response to the demand of the audience
28. Put out, throw out, or expel
29. Sneaky

Down

1. Feeling of regret for one's misdeeds or sins
2. Foot doctor
3. Entrance hall
4. One who gives aid, esp. financial aid
5. Swelled up
6. Word for word
7. Regrets
11. Unpleasant to taste or smell
13. Motionless
15. Intensity
16. Astounded; dazed
17. Dull
19. Escaped the understanding of
21. Became violently active; exploded
23. Real
24. Contrary to what is expected

Copyrighted

Joy Luck Club Vocabulary Crossword 2

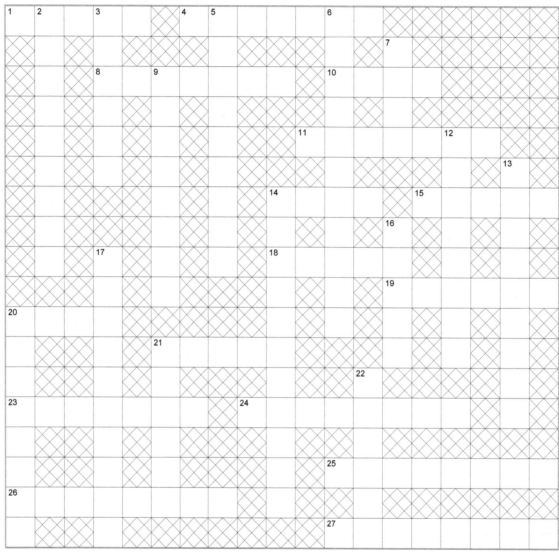

Across

1. Decreased
4. Swelled up
8. Mysteriously strange
10. Tight
11. Regrets
14. Dull
15. Royal
18. Abyss; gorge; steep-sided hole
19. Contrary to what is expected
20. Conceited; proud
21. Entrance hall
23. Street markets
24. Motionless
25. Great dislike
26. Arrogant; presumptuous and insulting
27. Bringing back to life

Down

2. Deserted; left
3. Escaped the understanding of
5. Length of life
6. Beyond necessary; luxurious
7. Speechless
9. Agreement
12. Study of religion
13. Quality of being impossible to control or repress
14. Statement
16. Offensively self-satisfied smile
17. One who gives aid, esp. financial aid
20. Word for word
21. Make a thorough search for
22. Performance in response to the demand of the audience

Copyrighted

1 W	2 A	N	3 E	D		4 B	5 L	O	A	T	6 E	D		
	B		L				O				X	7 M		
	A	8 U	N	9 C	A	N	N	Y		10 T	A	U	T	
	N	D		O		G				R		T		
	D	E		V		E		11 L	A	M	E	N	12 T	S
	O	D		E		V			V			H		13 S
	N			N		I	14 D	R	A	B	15 R	E	G	A	L
	E			A		T	E		G		16 S		O		U
	D	17 B	N		Y		18 C	H	A	S	M		L		C
		E	T				L		N		19 I	R	O	N	I	C
20 V	A	I	N				A		T		R		G		N
E		E	21 F	O	Y	E	R				K		Y		E
R		F	O				A		22 E						S
23 B	A	Z	A	A	R	S		24 S	T	A	G	N	A	N	T	S
A		C	A				I		C						
T		T	G				O		25 L	O	A	T	H	I	N	G
26 I	N	S	O	L	E	N	T		N		R				
M		R							27 R	E	V	I	V	I	N	G

Across

1. Decreased
4. Swelled up
8. Mysteriously strange
10. Tight
11. Regrets
14. Dull
15. Royal
18. Abyss; gorge; steep-sided hole
19. Contrary to what is expected
20. Conceited; proud
21. Entrance hall
23. Street markets
24. Motionless
25. Great dislike
26. Arrogant; presumptuous and insulting
27. Bringing back to life

Down

2. Deserted; left
3. Escaped the understanding of
5. Length of life
6. Beyond necessary; luxurious
7. Speechless
9. Agreement
12. Study of religion
13. Quality of being impossible to control or repress
14. Statement
16. Offensively self-satisfied smile
17. One who gives aid, esp. financial aid
20. Word for word
21. Make a thorough search for
22. Performance in response to the demand of the audience

Copyrighted

Joy Luck Club Vocabulary Crossword 3

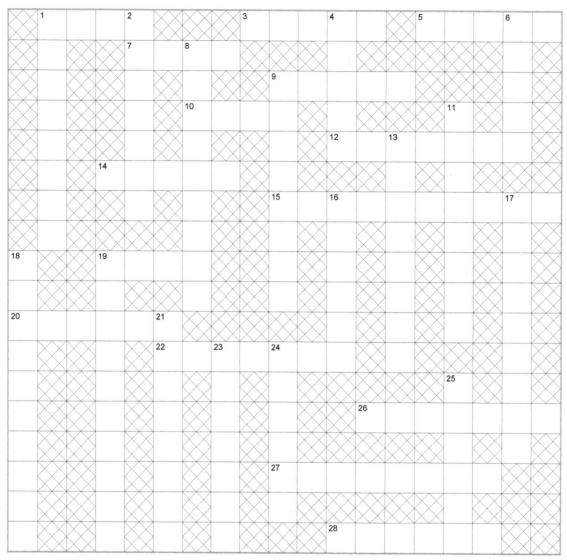

Across
1. Tight
3. Entrance hall
5. Royal
7. A crafty plan
9. Offensively self-satisfied smile
10. Speechless
12. Gradually smaller from one end to the other
14. Decreased
15. Unavoidable; bound to happen
19. Conceited; proud
20. Small or deficient in quantity
22. Became violently active; exploded
26. Regrets
27. Surrounded by something almost to the point of being lost in it
28. Person who carries baggage

Down
1. Study of religion
2. Of little importance
4. Put out, throw out, or expel
6. Unpleasant to taste or smell
8. Silly or self-conscious
9. Guard
11. Introductory occurrence or statement
13. In perfect condition
16. Escaped the understanding of
17. Length of life
18. Regretful; sorrowful
19. Done with force or energy
21. Left-overs
23. Mysteriously strange
24. Publicly praised
25. Treat with respect

Copyrighted

```
 1        2              3        4        5        6
 T  A  U  T        F  O  Y  E  R     R  E  G  A  L
    H        7R  U  8S  E           4V              6C
    E        I        I        9S  M  I  R  K        R
    O        V        10M  U  T  E        C     11P  I
    L        I        P        N        12T  A  13P  E  R  E  D
    O     14W  A  N  E  D        T           R     E
    G        L        I     15I  N  16E  V  I  T  A  B  17L  E
    Y        I        N        L        S     M     O
18R        19V  A  I  N        E        U     T  B  N
 E        I           G        L        D     I  L  G
20M  E  A  G  E  21R           E        N     E     E
 O        O     22E  R  23U  24P  T  E  D     E     V
 R        R     M     N     O           25R     I
 S        O     N     C     U        26L  A  M  E  N  T  S
 E        U     A     A     T              V     Y
 F        S     N     N  27E  N  G  U  L  F  E  D
 U        L     T     N     D              R
 L        Y     S     Y     28P  O  R  T  E  R
```

Across

1. Tight
3. Entrance hall
5. Royal
7. A crafty plan
9. Offensively self-satisfied smile
10. Speechless
12. Gradually smaller from one end to the other
14. Decreased
15. Unavoidable; bound to happen
19. Conceited; proud
20. Small or deficient in quantity
22. Became violently active; exploded
26. Regrets
27. Surrounded by something almost to the point of being lost in it
28. Person who carries baggage

Down

1. Study of religion
2. Of little importance
4. Put out, throw out, or expel
6. Unpleasant to taste or smell
8. Silly or self-conscious
9. Guard
11. Introductory occurrence or statement
13. In perfect condition
16. Escaped the understanding of
17. Length of life
18. Regretful; sorrowful
19. Done with force or energy
21. Left-overs
23. Mysteriously strange
24. Publicly praised
25. Treat with respect

Copyrighted

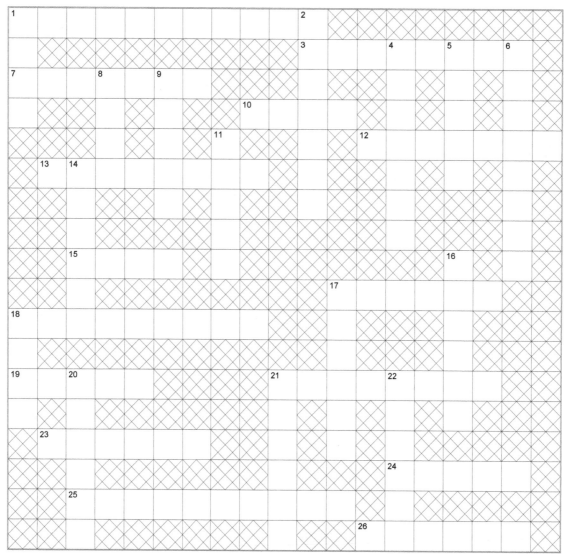

Across

1. Hypnotizing
3. Surrounded by something almost to the point of being lost in it
7. Of little importance
10. Tight
12. Regrets
13. Guard
15. Dull
17. Serious
18. Departing from the norm; extremely
19. Offensively self-satisfied smile
21. Scampered; hurried along
23. Person who carries baggage
24. Put out, throw out, or expel
25. Unavoidable; bound to happen
26. Skillfully

Down

1. Speechless
2. Real
4. Mysteriously strange
5. Entrance hall
6. Divert
8. Conceited; proud
9. Unpleasant to taste or smell
11. Royal
14. Escaped the understanding of
16. Small or deficient in quantity
17. Husband or wife
18. A crafty plan
20. Contrary to what is expected
21. Of substandard quality
22. Treat with respect

Copyrighted

¹M	E	S	M	E	R	I	Z	I	N	²G		
U										³E	N	G
⁷T	R	⁸I	V	⁹I	A	L				N		N
E		A		C			¹⁰T	A	U	T		C
		I		R		¹¹R		I			¹²L	A
¹³S	¹⁴E	N	T	I	N	E	L		N		N	
	L		D		G			E		N		R
	U		A		Y					Y		C
¹⁵D	R	A	B		L			¹⁶M		T		
E						¹⁷S	O	M	B	E	R	
¹⁸R	A	D	I	C	A	L	L	Y		P		A
U						O				G		
¹⁹S	M	²⁰I	R	K		²¹S	C	U	R	²²R	I	E D
E		R				H		S		E		R
²³P	O	R	T	E	R		A		E		V	
		N				B		²⁴E	V	I	C	T
²⁵I	N	E	V	I	T	A	B	L	E		R	
		C				Y		²⁶D	E	F	T	L Y

Across

1. Hypnotizing
3. Surrounded by something almost to the point of being lost in it
7. Of little importance
10. Tight
12. Regrets
13. Guard
15. Dull
17. Serious
18. Departing from the norm; extremely
19. Offensively self-satisfied smile
21. Scampered; hurried along
23. Person who carries baggage
24. Put out, throw out, or expel
25. Unavoidable; bound to happen
26. Skillfully

Down

1. Speechless
2. Real
4. Mysteriously strange
5. Entrance hall
6. Divert
8. Conceited; proud
9. Unpleasant to taste or smell
11. Royal
14. Escaped the understanding of
16. Small or deficient in quantity
17. Husband or wife
18. A crafty plan
20. Contrary to what is expected
21. Of substandard quality
22. Treat with respect

Copyrighted

Joy Luck Club Vocabulary Juggle Letters 1

1. EERRVE   = 1. _____
                           Treat with respect

2. ARBMEEPL   = 2. _____
                           Introductory occurrence or statement

3. EBACIDSEPL   = 3. _____
                           Deserving strong dislike; vile

4. IGEEUNN   = 4. _____
                           Real

5. YAICLDRLA   = 5. _____
                           Departing from the norm; extremely

6. UNACSSESI   = 6. _____
                           Quality of being impossible to control or repress

7. ULINOLSI   = 7. _____
                           False perception of reality

8. AVRNTATXGAE   = 8. _____
                           Beyond necessary; luxurious

9. BLBIANBG   = 9. _____
                           Talking in nonsense

10. ETLDFY   =10. _____
                           Skillfully

11. MATVRIEB   =11. _____
                           Word for word

12. ASSTCIEH   =12. _____
                           Criticize; punish; reprimand

13. IIPASRODTT   =13. _____
                           Foot doctor

14. TUEM   =14. _____
                           Speechless

15. SRANTPARETN   =15. _____
                           Clear

Copyrighted

1. EERRVE

2. ARBMEEPL

3. EBACIDSEPL

4. IGEEUNN

5. YAICLDRLA

6. UNACSSESI

7. ULINOLSI

8. AVRNTATXGAE

9. BLBIANBG

10. ETLDFY

11. MATVRIEB

12. ASSTCIEH

13. IIPASRODTT

14. TUEM

15. SRANTPARETN

= 1. REVERE
Treat with respect

= 2. PREAMBLE
Introductory occurrence or statement

= 3. DESPICABLE
Deserving strong dislike; vile

= 4. GENUINE
Real

= 5. RADICALLY
Departing from the norm; extremely

= 6. SAUCINESS
Quality of being impossible to control or repress

= 7. ILLUSION
False perception of reality

= 8. EXTRAVAGANT
Beyond necessary; luxurious

= 9. BABBLING
Talking in nonsense

=10. DEFTLY
Skillfully

=11. VERBATIM
Word for word

=12. CHASTISE
Criticize; punish; reprimand

=13. PODIATRIST
Foot doctor

=14. MUTE
Speechless

=15. TRANSPARENT
Clear

Copyrighted

1. ODRPGIY   = 1. _____

Person with exceptional talents

2. OSREPTCP   = 2. _____

Something expected

3. MEASTNL   = 3. _____

Regrets

4. LGRSIOUVYO   = 4. _____

Done with force or energy

5. SLEPCIDBAE   = 5. _____

Deserving strong dislike; vile

6. ASRAABZ   = 6. _____

Street markets

7. SUER   = 7. _____

A crafty plan

8. ICSTHEAS   = 8. _____

Criticize; punish; reprimand

9. MRESNTNA   = 9. _____

Left-overs

10. NTIESLEN   =10. _____

Guard

11. VGIREVNI   =11. _____

Bringing back to life

12. TMUE   =12. _____

Speechless

13. OIYSALNMUNU =13. _____

Completely in agreement

14. VTULEATIC   =14. _____

Grow; encourage; promote

15. SHCMA   =15. _____

Abyss; gorge; steep-sided hole

Copyrighted

1. ODRPGIY

= 1. PRODIGY

Person with exceptional talents

2. OSREPTCP

= 2. PROSPECT

Something expected

3. MEASTNL

= 3. LAMENTS

Regrets

4. LGRSIOUVYO

= 4. VIGOROUSLY

Done with force or energy

5. SLEPCIDBAE

= 5. DESPICABLE

Deserving strong dislike; vile

6. ASRAABZ

= 6. BAZAARS

Street markets

7. SUER

= 7. RUSE

A crafty plan

8. ICSTHEAS

= 8. CHASTISE

Criticize; punish; reprimand

9. MRESNTNA

= 9. REMNANTS

Left-overs

10. NTIESLEN

=10. SENTINEL

Guard

11. VGIREVNI

=11. REVIVING

Bringing back to life

12. TMUE

=12. MUTE

Speechless

13. OIYSALNMUNU

=13. UNANIMOUSLY

Completely in agreement

14. VTULEATIC

=14. CULTIVATE

Grow; encourage; promote

15. SHCMA

=15. CHASM

Abyss; gorge; steep-sided hole

Copyrighted

1. LEGTOYHO   = 1. _____
   Study of religion

2. EUTTOD   = 2. _____
   Publicly praised

3. LGREA   = 3. _____
   Royal

4. MRRLEFUOSE   = 4. _____
   Regretful; sorrowful

5. TBLDOAE   = 5. _____
   Swelled up

6. BEPEARML   = 6. _____
   Introductory occurrence or statement

7. TUEREPD   = 7. _____
   Became violently active; exploded

8. BEIAIVLNTE   = 8. _____
   Unavoidable; bound to happen

9. LIVTIRA   = 9. _____
   Of little importance

10. RNEOCE   =10. _____
   Performance in response to the demand of the audience

11. EARNTNSM   =11. _____
   Left-overs

12. ODRYW   =12. _____
   Money or property brought by a bride to her new husband

13. HSSCITEA   =13. _____
   Criticize; punish; reprimand

14. SASSENCIU   =14. _____
   Quality of being impossible to control or repress

15. UCSEDRIR   =15. _____
   Scampered; hurried along

Copyrighted

1. LEGTOYHO = 1. THEOLOGY
Study of religion

2. EUTTOD = 2. TOUTED
Publicly praised

3. LGREA = 3. REGAL
Royal

4. MRRLEFUOSE = 4. REMORSEFUL
Regretful; sorrowful

5. TBLDOAE = 5. BLOATED
Swelled up

6. BEPEARML = 6. PREAMBLE
Introductory occurrence or statement

7. TUEREPD = 7. ERUPTED
Became violently active; exploded

8. BEIAIVLNTE = 8. INEVITABLE
Unavoidable; bound to happen

9. LIVTIRA = 9. TRIVIAL
Of little importance

10. RNEOCE =10. ENCORE
Performance in response to the demand of the audience

11. EARNTNSM =11. REMNANTS
Left-overs

12. ODRYW =12. DOWRY
Money or property brought by a bride to her new husband

13. HSSCITEA =13. CHASTISE
Criticize; punish; reprimand

14. SASSENCIU =14. SAUCINESS
Quality of being impossible to control or repress

15. UCSEDRIR =15. SCURRIED
Scampered; hurried along

Copyrighted

1. INESIMRMG   = 1. _____
Cooking just below the boiling point

2. TAETEPRNE   = 2. _____
Pierce; force into

3. ONADPR   = 3. _____
Forgive

4. GREAME   = 4. _____
Small or deficient in quantity

5. NERPSITI   = 5. _____
In perfect condition

6. TEISHCSA   = 6. _____
Criticize; punish; reprimand

7. MSEATNL   = 7. _____
Regrets

8. UEOSDIV   = 8. _____
Sneaky

9. EERLMRUOSF   = 9. _____
Regretful; sorrowful

10. SNEOILTN   =10. _____
Arrogant; presumptuous and insulting

11. LIUOLNSI   =11. _____
False perception of reality

12. AROGFE   =12. _____
Make a thorough search for

13. INCUGNN   =13. _____
Deceitful cleverness

14. SPROCTEP   =14. _____
Something expected

15. UPSEOS   =15. _____
Husband or wife

Copyrighted

1. INESIMRMG

   = 1. SIMMERING

       Cooking just below the boiling point

2. TAETEPRNE

   = 2. PENETRATE

       Pierce; force into

3. ONADPR

   = 3. PARDON

       Forgive

4. GREAME

   = 4. MEAGER

       Small or deficient in quantity

5. NERPSITI

   = 5. PRISTINE

       In perfect condition

6. TEISHCSA

   = 6. CHASTISE

       Criticize; punish; reprimand

7. MSEATNL

   = 7. LAMENTS

       Regrets

8. UEOSDIV

   = 8. DEVIOUS

       Sneaky

9. EERLMRUOSF

   = 9. REMORSEFUL

       Regretful; sorrowful

10. SNEOILTN

   =10. INSOLENT

       Arrogant; presumptuous and insulting

11. LIUOLNSI

   =11. ILLUSION

       False perception of reality

12. AROGFE

   =12. FORAGE

       Make a thorough search for

13. INCUGNN

   =13. CUNNING

       Deceitful cleverness

14. SPROCTEP

   =14. PROSPECT

       Something expected

15. UPSEOS

   =15. SPOUSE

       Husband or wife

Copyrighted

ABANDONED	Deserted; left
ACRID	Unpleasant to taste or smell
BABBLING	Talking in nonsense
BAZAARS	Street markets
BELLOWS	Very loud, deep sounds
BENEFACTOR	One who gives aid, esp. financial aid
BENEVOLENT	Characterized by being or doing good

Copyrighted

BLOATED	Swelled up
CANOPY	Roof-like covering
CAUTIOUSLY	Carefully
CHASM	Abyss; gorge; steep-sided hole
CHASTISE	Criticize; punish; reprimand
CICADAS	Insects that make high-pitched, droning sound
COVENANT	Agreement

Copyrighted

CULTIVATE	Grow; encourage; promote
CUNNING	Deceitful cleverness
DECLARATION	Statement
DEFTLY	Skillfully
DESPICABLE	Deserving strong dislike; vile
DEVIOUS	Sneaky
DISTRACT	Divert

Copyrighted

DOWRY	Money or property brought by a bride to her new husband
DRAB	Dull
ELUDED	Escaped the understanding of
ENCORE	Performance in response to the demand of the audience
ENGULFED	Surrounded by something almost to the point of being lost in it
ERUPTED	Became violently active; exploded
EVICT	Put out, throw out, or expel

Copyrighted

EXASPERATED	At the end of patience; irritated
EXTRACTED	Pulled out
EXTRAVAGANT	Beyond necessary; luxurious
FORAGE	Make a thorough search for
FOYER	Entrance hall
GENUINE	Real
ILLUSION	False perception of reality

Copyrighted

INEVITABLE	Unavoidable; bound to happen
INSOLENT	Arrogant; presumptuous and insulting
INVADED	Entered by force to conquer
INVENTORY	Taking a count of
IRONIC	Contrary to what is expected
IRRATIONAL	Not reasonable
IRREVOCABLE	Can't be changed back

Copyrighted

LAMENTS	Regrets
LOATHING	Great dislike
LONGEVITY	Length of life
MEAGER	Small or deficient in quantity
MESMERIZING	Hypnotizing
MUTE	Speechless
OBSESSING	Thinking continually about something

Copyrighted

PARANOID	Having an extreme fear or distrust of others
PARDON	Forgive
PENETRATE	Pierce; force into
PODIATRIST	Foot doctor
PORTER	Person who carries baggage
POSTERITY	Future generations
PREAMBLE	Introductory occurrence or statement

Copyrighted

PRECIOUS	Cherished; having value; beloved
PRESUMPTUOUS	Excessively forward
PRETENSE	False appearance
PRISTINE	In perfect condition
PRODIGY	Person with exceptional talents
PROSPECT	Something expected
RADICALLY	Departing from the norm; extremely

Copyrighted

REGAL	Royal
REMNANTS	Left-overs
REMORSE	Feeling of regret for one's misdeeds or sins
REMORSEFUL	Regretful; sorrowful
REVERE	Treat with respect
REVIVING	Bringing back to life
RUSE	A crafty plan

Copyrighted

SAUCINESS	Quality of being impossible to control or repress
SCHEMING	Plotting to achieve an evil or illegal end
SCURRIED	Scampered; hurried along
SENTINEL	Guard
SHABBY	Of substandard quality
SIMMERING	Cooking just below the boiling point
SIMPERING	Silly or self-conscious

Copyrighted

SMIRK	Offensively self-satisfied smile
SOMBER	Serious
SPOUSE	Husband or wife
STAGNANT	Motionless
STRATEGY	Plan
STUNNED	Astounded; dazed
SURVEYED	Looked over

Copyrighted

TAPERED	Gradually smaller from one end to the other
TAUT	Tight
THEOLOGY	Study of religion
TOUTED	Publicly praised
TRANSLUCENT	Allowing some light to pass through
TRANSPARENT	Clear
TRIVIAL	Of little importance

Copyrighted

UNANIMOUSLY	Completely in agreement
UNCANNY	Mysteriously strange
VAIN	Conceited; proud
VEHEMENCE	Intensity
VERBATIM	Word for word
VIGOROUSLY	Done with force or energy
VULNERABLE	Able to be hurt

Copyrighted

WANED

Decreased

Copyrighted

Joy Luck Club Vocabulary

PODIATRIST	ELUDED	IRRATIONAL	OBSESSING	SAUCINESS
CUNNING	VIGOROUSLY	LONGEVITY	TAUT	CANOPY
STAGNANT	LAMENTS	FREE SPACE	VEHEMENCE	CHASM
PRISTINE	THEOLOGY	EXTRAVAGANT	POSTERITY	VAIN
ABANDONED	TRIVIAL	INEVITABLE	TRANSLUCENT	REGAL

Joy Luck Club Vocabulary

SCURRIED	ILLUSION	SIMPERING	STUNNED	EVICT
CHASTISE	SENTINEL	VULNERABLE	CULTIVATE	COVENANT
BLOATED	TAPERED	FREE SPACE	INSOLENT	RUSE
EXTRACTED	BELLOWS	FOYER	INVENTORY	DRAB
MUTE	IRREVOCABLE	UNCANNY	SPOUSE	PENETRATE

Copyrighted

Joy Luck Club Vocabulary

DEVIOUS	CAUTIOUSLY	COVENANT	LONGEVITY	INEVITABLE
PRECIOUS	PRETENSE	CUNNING	INVADED	REVERE
STUNNED	SOMBER	FREE SPACE	BELLOWS	POSTERITY
RUSE	BAZAARS	TOUTED	FOYER	CHASM
THEOLOGY	MESMERIZING	PROSPECT	VIGOROUSLY	BENEVOLENT

Joy Luck Club Vocabulary

WANED	ENGULFED	EXASPERATED	TRANSPARENT	TAUT
TAPERED	DISTRACT	ERUPTED	SHABBY	PARDON
SMIRK	TRIVIAL	FREE SPACE	IRREVOCABLE	VEHEMENCE
REMORSEFUL	SCURRIED	ILLUSION	SCHEMING	DOWRY
PARANOID	BLOATED	LOATHING	TRANSLUCENT	LAMENTS

Copyrighted

Joy Luck Club Vocabulary

VEHEMENCE	ENCORE	BLOATED	CAUTIOUSLY	PODIATRIST
DECLARATION	CULTIVATE	INVADED	TAPERED	OBSESSING
SHABBY	DRAB	FREE SPACE	BENEVOLENT	CANOPY
VERBATIM	SIMMERING	EVICT	STUNNED	THEOLOGY
SENTINEL	ABANDONED	UNANIMOUSLY	RADICALLY	CUNNING

Joy Luck Club Vocabulary

WANED	MUTE	SOMBER	PROSPECT	BAZAARS
LOATHING	SIMPERING	REVIVING	SPOUSE	SCHEMING
TRANSLUCENT	ERUPTED	FREE SPACE	CICADAS	PRESUMPTUOUS
PRISTINE	TOUTED	REGAL	INVENTORY	GENUINE
PRODIGY	INSOLENT	PARDON	PREAMBLE	VAIN

Copyrighted

Joy Luck Club Vocabulary

PENETRATE	INEVITABLE	PARDON	VERBATIM	SCHEMING
CICADAS	DEVIOUS	INVENTORY	TOUTED	TAUT
CHASTISE	PODIATRIST	FREE SPACE	ELUDED	SIMMERING
PRISTINE	EXTRACTED	ACRID	PRODIGY	POSTERITY
CHASM	REMORSEFUL	VULNERABLE	BELLOWS	OBSESSING

Joy Luck Club Vocabulary

UNANIMOUSLY	DISTRACT	VAIN	SPOUSE	CULTIVATE
INSOLENT	IRREVOCABLE	PREAMBLE	MEAGER	ABANDONED
MUTE	THEOLOGY	FREE SPACE	BENEVOLENT	MESMERIZING
BABBLING	SENTINEL	FOYER	BAZAARS	DECLARATION
FORAGE	VIGOROUSLY	SMIRK	REVIVING	CUNNING

Copyrighted

Joy Luck Club Vocabulary

SIMMERING	FORAGE	RUSE	SHABBY	LOATHING
PORTER	EXASPERATED	REVIVING	ERUPTED	PODIATRIST
INVENTORY	LAMENTS	FREE SPACE	UNANIMOUSLY	ILLUSION
BELLOWS	INEVITABLE	VULNERABLE	SURVEYED	VEHEMENCE
PREAMBLE	ABANDONED	PRETENSE	SENTINEL	STRATEGY

Joy Luck Club Vocabulary

BABBLING	BAZAARS	INVADED	PARANOID	BENEVOLENT
MEAGER	STUNNED	DEVIOUS	DOWRY	STAGNANT
EXTRACTED	OBSESSING	FREE SPACE	PRECIOUS	PARDON
ENGULFED	CULTIVATE	CHASTISE	TRIVIAL	TRANSPARENT
ENCORE	MESMERIZING	IRREVOCABLE	TAUT	ELUDED

Copyrighted

Joy Luck Club Vocabulary

PRISTINE	BELLOWS	EXTRACTED	CUNNING	STUNNED
PRECIOUS	OBSESSING	ABANDONED	MUTE	THEOLOGY
UNCANNY	ERUPTED	FREE SPACE	TRANSLUCENT	UNANIMOUSLY
VEHEMENCE	SIMPERING	EXTRAVAGANT	PARDON	DEVIOUS
SHABBY	REVERE	LAMENTS	IRREVOCABLE	RUSE

Joy Luck Club Vocabulary

DOWRY	INSOLENT	VIGOROUSLY	PRODIGY	PARANOID
MESMERIZING	VULNERABLE	TOUTED	RADICALLY	CHASTISE
PREAMBLE	INEVITABLE	FREE SPACE	TAUT	DESPICABLE
STAGNANT	MEAGER	COVENANT	SOMBER	PODIATRIST
DISTRACT	DECLARATION	FOYER	WANED	REMORSEFUL

Copyrighted

Joy Luck Club Vocabulary

SPOUSE	INVENTORY	ILLUSION	LOATHING	SCURRIED
VAIN	ACRID	CANOPY	SURVEYED	BENEFACTOR
SIMPERING	CHASTISE	FREE SPACE	INSOLENT	EXTRAVAGANT
UNANIMOUSLY	GENUINE	MEAGER	INVADED	IRREVOCABLE
BABBLING	PRECIOUS	IRRATIONAL	STAGNANT	UNCANNY

Joy Luck Club Vocabulary

PORTER	THEOLOGY	RADICALLY	SCHEMING	REMORSE
TAPERED	PARDON	INEVITABLE	PRESUMPTUOUS	POSTERITY
CUNNING	DRAB	FREE SPACE	REMNANTS	REVIVING
ELUDED	PRISTINE	SENTINEL	WANED	COVENANT
REGAL	ENGULFED	FOYER	LAMENTS	EXASPERATED

Copyrighted

Joy Luck Club Vocabulary

SURVEYED	CHASM	REGAL	SIMPERING	CICADAS
EXTRACTED	VEHEMENCE	REVERE	ELUDED	PRECIOUS
EXASPERATED	PODIATRIST	FREE SPACE	STAGNANT	BENEVOLENT
INEVITABLE	GENUINE	LONGEVITY	RADICALLY	CULTIVATE
UNANIMOUSLY	BELLOWS	REMORSE	SCURRIED	INVADED

Joy Luck Club Vocabulary

BLOATED	BENEFACTOR	SENTINEL	IRRATIONAL	TRIVIAL
ENCORE	DEFTLY	TRANSLUCENT	OBSESSING	COVENANT
FOYER	REMORSEFUL	FREE SPACE	CAUTIOUSLY	ACRID
SIMMERING	LAMENTS	LOATHING	CUNNING	INSOLENT
PARDON	ILLUSION	VERBATIM	DISTRACT	POSTERITY

Copyrighted

Joy Luck Club Vocabulary

DISTRACT	ERUPTED	REMORSE	ILLUSION	DEVIOUS
UNCANNY	WANED	ACRID	UNANIMOUSLY	PODIATRIST
EXTRAVAGANT	VERBATIM	FREE SPACE	LAMENTS	COVENANT
STAGNANT	VEHEMENCE	PROSPECT	LONGEVITY	CULTIVATE
RADICALLY	TAUT	TAPERED	REVERE	REMORSEFUL

Joy Luck Club Vocabulary

SENTINEL	POSTERITY	PREAMBLE	FOYER	TRANSLUCENT
MESMERIZING	VIGOROUSLY	SOMBER	VULNERABLE	ENGULFED
LOATHING	SIMPERING	FREE SPACE	DRAB	CANOPY
PRESUMPTUOUS	PRODIGY	STRATEGY	BLOATED	REVIVING
GENUINE	ABANDONED	STUNNED	SURVEYED	EXTRACTED

Copyrighted

Joy Luck Club Vocabulary

ENCORE	THEOLOGY	EXASPERATED	IRRATIONAL	FORAGE
SIMMERING	DEFTLY	SPOUSE	TOUTED	IRREVOCABLE
REVIVING	VEHEMENCE	FREE SPACE	UNCANNY	CANOPY
BENEVOLENT	STUNNED	PENETRATE	SCURRIED	LONGEVITY
SAUCINESS	RUSE	TAPERED	PREAMBLE	PROSPECT

Joy Luck Club Vocabulary

REVERE	LAMENTS	CHASM	ENGULFED	WANED
REGAL	DECLARATION	PARANOID	BLOATED	REMORSEFUL
TRANSLUCENT	TAUT	FREE SPACE	STRATEGY	FOYER
REMNANTS	CUNNING	PODIATRIST	PRODIGY	PORTER
VULNERABLE	MUTE	SIMPERING	CHASTISE	BELLOWS

Copyrighted

Joy Luck Club Vocabulary

SIMMERING	PARANOID	IRREVOCABLE	BAZAARS	MESMERIZING
POSTERITY	LOATHING	DOWRY	ACRID	CHASTISE
EXASPERATED	ENGULFED	FREE SPACE	DISTRACT	CAUTIOUSLY
PORTER	RADICALLY	TOUTED	PROSPECT	INSOLENT
ABANDONED	LAMENTS	SURVEYED	PRESUMPTUOUS	GENUINE

Joy Luck Club Vocabulary

INEVITABLE	TRIVIAL	IRRATIONAL	MEAGER	DEFTLY
REVIVING	PREAMBLE	SAUCINESS	VIGOROUSLY	THEOLOGY
DESPICABLE	SHABBY	FREE SPACE	EVICT	BENEVOLENT
DECLARATION	DRAB	BELLOWS	INVENTORY	PRETENSE
SPOUSE	TRANSLUCENT	REMORSE	CHASM	INVADED

Copyrighted

Joy Luck Club Vocabulary

THEOLOGY	REMNANTS	REVIVING	PROSPECT	PARANOID
PRECIOUS	MUTE	WANED	IRONIC	CICADAS
ENCORE	RADICALLY	FREE SPACE	SAUCINESS	ILLUSION
CUNNING	FORAGE	LONGEVITY	PENETRATE	BLOATED
GENUINE	SPOUSE	EXTRACTED	DRAB	LAMENTS

Joy Luck Club Vocabulary

BENEVOLENT	TRANSPARENT	SOMBER	COVENANT	IRREVOCABLE
UNCANNY	RUSE	DEFTLY	SENTINEL	BELLOWS
ABANDONED	TAUT	FREE SPACE	SHABBY	DISTRACT
TRIVIAL	CHASTISE	FOYER	SURVEYED	EXTRAVAGANT
STRATEGY	VEHEMENCE	CHASM	PORTER	CULTIVATE

Copyrighted

Joy Luck Club Vocabulary

DOWRY	PRISTINE	FORAGE	LOATHING	SIMMERING
CULTIVATE	REVIVING	IRREVOCABLE	PRESUMPTUOUS	UNCANNY
ACRID	INVADED	FREE SPACE	TRIVIAL	DEFTLY
SIMPERING	BENEVOLENT	STAGNANT	VERBATIM	SCURRIED
MESMERIZING	RADICALLY	MUTE	PODIATRIST	ENGULFED

Joy Luck Club Vocabulary

ENCORE	FOYER	GENUINE	SENTINEL	REGAL
VIGOROUSLY	ELUDED	UNANIMOUSLY	REMORSEFUL	EXTRACTED
IRONIC	RUSE	FREE SPACE	ABANDONED	LAMENTS
SAUCINESS	WANED	INEVITABLE	BELLOWS	PRECIOUS
INSOLENT	BAZAARS	THEOLOGY	PRODIGY	POSTERITY

Copyrighted

Joy Luck Club Vocabulary

REMNANTS	STRATEGY	SCHEMING	IRONIC	INVENTORY
FOYER	VULNERABLE	RUSE	COVENANT	ENGULFED
INVADED	ILLUSION	FREE SPACE	BELLOWS	SCURRIED
SURVEYED	DRAB	REMORSEFUL	RADICALLY	MEAGER
VERBATIM	LOATHING	EVICT	FORAGE	ACRID

Joy Luck Club Vocabulary

TRANSPARENT	CAUTIOUSLY	BAZAARS	TAPERED	DISTRACT
EXASPERATED	ABANDONED	SHABBY	SPOUSE	PARDON
PRISTINE	SMIRK	FREE SPACE	UNCANNY	BENEFACTOR
TOUTED	PRECIOUS	DESPICABLE	DEFTLY	POSTERITY
TRIVIAL	CHASTISE	WANED	PRESUMPTUOUS	IRRATIONAL

Copyrighted

Joy Luck Club Vocabulary

DESPICABLE	SHABBY	DECLARATION	PRESUMPTUOUS	CAUTIOUSLY
VAIN	VIGOROUSLY	LONGEVITY	BENEVOLENT	ACRID
EXTRAVAGANT	SIMMERING	FREE SPACE	RUSE	PRECIOUS
EXASPERATED	CHASTISE	PENETRATE	TOUTED	RADICALLY
PROSPECT	ENCORE	CANOPY	INVADED	MEAGER

Joy Luck Club Vocabulary

ERUPTED	SCURRIED	CICADAS	REMORSE	INSOLENT
SENTINEL	LAMENTS	UNCANNY	REVERE	BABBLING
EXTRACTED	PRISTINE	FREE SPACE	EVICT	OBSESSING
SURVEYED	MUTE	PORTER	IRREVOCABLE	SOMBER
DEFTLY	WANED	CUNNING	VEHEMENCE	PARANOID

Copyrighted

Joy Luck Club Vocabulary

STRATEGY	PROSPECT	CHASTISE	RUSE	VAIN
BAZAARS	SCHEMING	VIGOROUSLY	EXTRAVAGANT	IRREVOCABLE
SPOUSE	SIMPERING	FREE SPACE	SOMBER	PENETRATE
OBSESSING	PARDON	THEOLOGY	CICADAS	TOUTED
LAMENTS	VEHEMENCE	PRODIGY	DEFTLY	REMORSEFUL

Joy Luck Club Vocabulary

IRRATIONAL	BELLOWS	COVENANT	ACRID	MUTE
SURVEYED	BENEVOLENT	ILLUSION	DESPICABLE	BLOATED
ERUPTED	DECLARATION	FREE SPACE	PARANOID	EXASPERATED
SAUCINESS	EXTRACTED	REMORSE	REGAL	RADICALLY
REVIVING	TAUT	PODIATRIST	MESMERIZING	INVENTORY

Copyrighted